Archangel Michael

Connecting with the Angel of the Lord

© Copyright 2024 - All rights reserved.

The content contained within this book may not be reproduced, duplicated, or transmitted without direct written permission from the author or the publisher.

Under no circumstances will any blame or legal responsibility be held against the publisher, or author, for any damages, reparation, or monetary loss due to the information contained within this book, either directly or indirectly.

Legal Notice:

This book is copyright protected. It is only for personal use. You cannot amend, distribute, sell, use, quote, or paraphrase any part of the content within this book without the consent of the author or publisher.

Disclaimer Notice:

Please note the information contained within this document is for educational and entertainment purposes only. All effort has been executed to present accurate, up-to-date, reliable, and complete information. No warranties of any kind are declared or implied. Readers acknowledge that the author is not engaging in the rendering of legal, financial, medical, or professional advice. The content within this book has been derived from various sources. Please consult a licensed professional before attempting any techniques outlined in this book.

By reading this document, the reader agrees that under no circumstances is the author responsible for any losses, direct or indirect, that are incurred as a result of the use of the information contained within this document, including, but not limited to, errors, omissions, or inaccuracies.

Your Free Gift
(only available for a limited time)

Thanks for getting this book! If you want to learn more about various spirituality topics, then join Mari Silva's community and get a free guided meditation MP3 for awakening your third eye. This guided meditation mp3 is designed to open and strengthen ones third eye so you can experience a higher state of consciousness. Simply visit the link below the image to get started.

https://spiritualityspot.com/meditation

Table of Contents

INTRODUCTION 1
CHAPTER 1: WHO IS ARCHANGEL MICHAEL? 3
CHAPTER 2: HOW TO CALL UPON ARCHANGEL MICHAEL 14
CHAPTER 3: SIGNS THAT ARCHANGEL MICHAEL IS PRESENT 24
CHAPTER 4: REQUESTING PROTECTION 32
CHAPTER 5: REQUESTING HEALING 43
CHAPTER 6: BANISHING NEGATIVE ENERGY 54
CHAPTER 7: CRYSTALS TO CONNECT WITH ARCHANGEL MICHAEL 65
CHAPTER 8: HERBS AND ESSENTIAL OILS OF ARCHANGEL MICHAEL 75
CHAPTER 9: DAILY RITUALS 85
BONUS: CORRESPONDENCES SHEET 95
CONCLUSION 103
HERE'S ANOTHER BOOK BY MARI SILVA THAT YOU MIGHT LIKE.. 105
YOUR FREE GIFT (ONLY AVAILABLE FOR A LIMITED TIME) 106
REFERENCES 107

Introduction

As the most powerful of Archangels, Michael can provide an enormous boost to your spirituality. Known as the "Angel of the Lord," Michael stands closer to the creator than any other Archangel. He commands all the other Archangels and an army of other angels. That should tell you exactly how much power he can lend you if needed. Suppose you want to deepen your spirituality and require protection from malicious intentions, cut out toxic influences from your life, expand your self-confidence and faith, and protect your space and your loved ones. In that case, Archangel Michael is the angel to connect with. However, to obtain any or all of this, you'll need to establish and nurture a personal connection with Michael; this is where the information you'll learn from this book will come in handy.

The book offers a comprehensive insight into who Archangel Michael is and the many ways you can communicate with him. To communicate with him efficiently, you must learn to recognize the signs he is sending you and decipher their messages. Once you familiarize yourself with his signs after reading the relevant chapter, you can delve into the specific request you wish to make. The first chapter will provide plenty of beginner-friendly methods for requesting Michael's protection for different occasions, like meditations and rituals. This will be followed by a chapter detailing how to request healing (through prayer, mediation, and harnessing the angel's light) and another chapter on asking for help in banishing negative energy from yourself, space, and others.

The tools you use when communicating with Archangel Michael can enhance your energy, allowing you to tap into his power more efficiently and manifest your intention faster and more accurately. Besides blue light, Michael is also associated with certain crystals (and their vibrations), herbs, and essential oils. Each of these elements carries its own energy, which can empower your own energy and increase the likelihood of manifesting your desires. The relevant chapters will show you which tools to use when requesting Michael's assistance. The last chapter will guide you in nurturing your bond with Archangel Michael through daily rituals, from wearing his colors to daily meditations and Reiki exercises. If you want to learn how to honor Archangel Michael throughout the year and what other tools you might use to call upon him, the bonus chapter will provide you with all his correspondences. It will act as a quick reference guide whenever you need something to use to establish and build a profound connection with Michael.

Archangel Michael is always there in times of distress, ready to take on any challenge and defend those in need – and this is no different with his modern-day followers. Independently of your cultural or religious background, Michael can help you reach spiritual fulfillment. After all, all you need is your willingness to connect with him, an open mind, and the ability to hone your intuition to recognize his messages. Throughout this book, you'll receive plenty of practical guidance for every aspect of working with this Archangel, from taking the first step of calling out to him to honoring him through regular practices. If you're ready to start your journey of building a beautiful and spiritually uplifting lifelong connection with Archangel Michael, continue reading.

Chapter 1: Who Is Archangel Michael?

Knowing that you aren't alone and angels constantly surround you is comforting. God created these heavenly creatures to serve Him and protect and guide humanity. You have probably experienced moments in your life when you felt that someone was watching over you, or you encountered events that were too strange to be considered coincidences. These are the angels at work. They always look out for you, send you messages, or change your direction to put you on the right track.

An icon of Archangel Michael in a cathedral.
Bielpincet, CC BY-SA 3.0 <https://creativecommons.org/licenses/by-sa/3.0>, via Wikimedia Commons https://commons.wikimedia.org/wiki/File:Icon_of_Archangel_Michael_in_Cathedral_in_the_name_of_Archangel_Michael.jpg

Archangels are the most powerful angels in Heaven. God entrusts them with significant tasks, and they have the freedom to travel to Earth to follow God's commands and help mankind. They hold the highest position in Heaven and are superior to all other angels.

The word "archangel" is derived from two Greek words: "arche," which means *ruler,* and "angelos," meaning *messenger.* The word represents their two responsibilities: the ruling of all angels and acting as messengers of God who deliver His messages to mankind. Archangels exist in all religions and spiritual beliefs.

There are four archangels in Islam and Judaism and seven in Christianity. This book will focus on the archangel Michael and in this chapter, you will learn everything about him, how he is represented in all three religions, and the symbols associated with him.

Introducing Archangel Michael

Michael is a leader and one of the main angels in Heaven. He is a strong and brave warrior who always fights on the side of good. He seeks to achieve justice and truth among all of mankind. Michael believes that evil will never prevail as long as people have faith in God. The angels are always on the side of the weak and helpless, protecting and defending them. People often call on Michael to give them the strength and courage to resist temptations, conquer their fears, and protect their hearts against straying from the right path. They also seek his help to heal the sick and ease their pain.

Michael is originally a Hebrew name that means "a gift from God." It is mentioned three times in the Book of Daniel from the Old Testament and once in the Quran. The name can also be spelled as Mikhail, Mikhael, Mikail, and Mikael. He is the only angel mentioned by name in the Quran, Bible, and the Torah.

Archangel Michael in the Bible and the Book of Daniel

Archangel Michael is described in the Book of Daniel as the "chief prince" of Heaven or the "great prince" who protected the people of Israel. He was mentioned without any introduction, and the book doesn't provide much information about him. This indicates that people were already familiar with him and knew who he was. The New Testament also doesn't give any details about Michael. When he was first mentioned, he and Satan were arguing over who would take Prophet Moses's dead body.

The Bible does not mention what Michael looks like, but he is often portrayed as a captain or a warrior. However, angels are often depicted as strong, beautiful, and tall beings. Mankind isn't equipped to see angels in their true form, so they usually appear in human form when they want to communicate directly with people to guide them or warn against impending doom. Therefore, scripture instructs believers to be kind and gracious to strangers since they can be angels in disguise.

Michael will play a big role in the fight against evil at the end of times. The Book of Daniel describes Michael as the protector of people who will rise to lead the angels in a war against Satan and his army of demons. The Book of Revelation tells us there will be a battle in Heaven, and Michael will fight a strong and vicious dragon. Both will have an army of angels by their side, but Michael will be victorious, and he will cast out the dragon from Heaven. The dragon and his army are Satan and his fallen angels.

In the Book of Enoch, Michael threw Satan and other fallen angels out of Heaven at the beginning of time. This wasn't mentioned in the Bible, but it is considered a prophecy of the battle that will take place in the future. Since Michael was able to get rid of Satan once, he will be able to do it again. The Bible states that good will triumph over evil, and Michael will win against Satan and his army.

Only Michael can defeat Satan because he always defends and protects believers from the devil and his demons.

He is also responsible for taking the souls of the dead believers to Heaven, and he will be the one to call on all mankind to come to life for Judgment Day.

Even though Michael isn't human, the church often refers to him as a saint. He is even celebrated and has his own feast, which takes place on September 29th. It is called Michaelmas, and people usually follow certain traditions to honor this day. For instance, they refrain from eating blackberries after the feast because when Michael threw Satan out of Heaven, he fell on a blackberry shrub. Ever since that day, all blackberries turn sour after Michaelmas in memory of Satan landing on them.

There is a misconception among Jehovah's Witnesses that Michael and Jesus Christ are the same person. They argue that since he is the protector of the people of Israel and the Bible also states that the Lord protects the children of Israel, they are the same. Michael is also described as "prince" in the Bible, and many believe this title only fits the son of God, Jesus Christ.

However, Michael is only a prince among the angels; his superiority doesn't extend to human beings. There are also six other archangels, so Michael isn't unique - unlike Jesus Christ, who is a prophet and the son of God.

Even though Michael is a powerful angel who always aids mankind, the Bible makes it clear that people should only worship God and pray to Him.

There are only a few mentions of Michael in the Bible which makes him one of the most fascinating and mysterious angels.

Archangel Michael in the Quran

In Islam, Michael is spelled as Mikhail or Mikail and is only mentioned once in the Quran:

> *"Who is an enemy to Allah, and His angels and His messengers, and Gabriel and Michael! Then, lo! Allah (Himself) is an enemy to the disbelievers."*

Even though this is the only mention of Michael and Allah didn't provide any other information on him, it is clear from this verse that he is held in high regard as he is mentioned with the Prophets, who are all dear to Allah. No other angel is mentioned in this verse, indicating that Michael and Gabriel are superior to all the other heavenly beings.

In Islam, Michael is responsible for the rain, plants, animals, human beings, and all-natural events. His job is to provide food for the body and the soul. He also appeared to Prophet Muhammad on more than one occasion. It was narrated in a hadith (a saying by Prophet Muhammad) that he once asked Gabriel why he had never seen Michael laugh. Gabriel said that Michael hadn't laughed since Hell was created.

The Quran tells the story of Prophet Muhammad's ascension to Heaven. Before he embarked on this journey, Michael and Gabriel prepared him by purifying his heart. The Prophet also said that both angels were his personal advisers.

Michael also cares about humanity and rewards believers for their kindness and good deeds. He is known for his mercy, and he often prays to God to forgive sinners and protect mosques and other places of worship. He and Gabriel will play a big role on Judgment Day. They will weigh each person's good and evil deeds, determining whether they will end up in Heaven or Hell.

In the Quran, when Allah created Adam, He ordered all angels to bow to Adam, and Gabriel and Michael were the first ones to follow His commands.

Archangel Michael in Spirituality and Other Beliefs

In Hinduism, Michael is described as the "Warrior Prince." He is the leader of the army of the gods and the defender of Dharma (the divine law in Hinduism). Some belief systems consider Michael a symbol of strength and hope rather than a protector and defender. Whether you are religious or not, you can benefit from having Michael in your life.

Nowadays, many people have lost hope, especially in the face of the injustice they face daily. They have given up and accepted that things will never get better. During these hard times, they need to look for something bigger than themselves. Michael became their light in their darkest days and their strength when they felt weak. In all religions and beliefs, Michael is a symbol of goodness, love, courage, dignity, strength, and other qualities people desperately need.

How Archangel Michael Can Help You

People often call on Michael more than any other angel. He can heal the sick, provide spiritual defense, and guide people to find meaning and purpose in their lives. He pushes them to discover who they really are and be loyal to their true selves. He can also raise their inner forces and psychic vibrations.

Michael is the first angel created by God, and he became in charge of dignity, truth, power, and security. He is often depicted with a sword that he uses to protect humanity from the devil.

Call on Michael whenever you struggle with self-esteem issues, lack energy, need direction, lack inspiration, or feel like you're under psychological attack. He can also help people who work in stressful jobs, struggle with nightmares, or have an addiction.

Find Meaning in Your Life

Call on Michael when you lack motivation; he will encourage you to become productive and organized and even find inspiration. Don't worry if you don't have what it takes to achieve your goals and realize your dreams. Michael will put you on the right track so you can acquire the necessary skills and talents to succeed in life and impact the world.

He will encourage you to create a routine so you can have a sense of stability in your life and thrive.

Comes Through During Tough Times

Don't hesitate to call on Michael if you are going through a tough time. He will come to your aid right away. Michael is always there for anyone in need. Whatever type of protection or help you require, he can provide it. All you have to do is ask. If you are in a tough situation and can't get through it alone, Michael will give you the strength and courage to overcome anything life throws at you.

Reassurance

Sometimes, you can feel alone, especially when you are about to make a big decision and aren't sure if it's right. Call on Michael, and he will reassure you that you aren't alone and that he is there, listening to you, and is aware of your struggles. He is watching over you and will encourage you to make the best decisions that will benefit you in the future.

Protects Your Energy

Empaths and highly sensitive individuals are easily affected by other people's energies. For instance, you have a friend who complains about everything. When you go out for lunch, they will complain about their job, relationship, the weather, their friends, and even the service at the restaurant. After spending a few hours with them, you return home feeling exhausted and depleted. Negative people are dangerous to empaths. They can drain your energy and make you feel tired and unable to do even the simplest of tasks. If these people are your co-workers and you meet them every day, this can severely damage your mental health.

Archangel Michael has the power to protect your energy from negative people. Every morning before you go to work, call on Michael to provide you with spiritual protection. If you are about to enter a place filled with negativity, ask the Archangel to clear the harmful energies from the place. If you share an office or a home with a negative person, ask him to watch over it and protect it when you are away.

You can even ask him to use his shield to protect you against negativity.

Provides You with Positivity

It is normal to be worried and scared if you are about to make a big decision, like getting married or changing your career. Stepping into the unknown is never easy. Michael will give you the courage to take the necessary risks. When things don't go your way and you lose hope, ask him to increase your positivity and optimism so you can keep going. He will show you that something good can always come out of every situation, even during moments when you feel like there is no hope.

Gives You Courage

There will be moments when you lose your self-esteem and feel scared and discouraged. For instance, your co-worker keeps taking credit for your work, or your boss dismisses all your ideas. Ask Michael to provide you with support and guidance to speak up for yourself and stand your ground. He can prepare you before talking to your boss and give you the confidence to say what is on your mind, even if your voice is shaking.

Michael can also help you with issues you are afraid to tackle, like aspects of your life that need changing or improving. For instance, your partner keeps crossing your boundaries, and you let them because you are afraid that they will leave you if you stand up for yourself. Or, you receive terrible news, feel lost, and struggle to accept it.

Remember that Michael is a warrior who can give you the courage and strength to face the unknown. Call on him to bestow his courage upon you so you feel confident enough to tackle these difficult situations. Michael won't only provide you with guidance, but he will also send you resources, opportunities, and even people who can help you. He will also make the journey easier by walking in front of you to fight battles you can't handle alone.

Protects You from Nightmares

Everyone has nightmares occasionally, but some people have realistic ones that wake them up feeling terrified in the middle of the night. Ask Michael to watch over you while you are sleeping or to scare away the nightmares using his mighty sword.

Your nightmares can stem from your subconscious. Perhaps you are worried about losing your job, or a family member is sick, and you are afraid they might not make it. These thoughts can keep you awake at night, and when you finally go to sleep, you end up having nightmares. If you call on Michael, he will cover you with his wings all night to make you feel comfortable and safe.

Cuts the Energetic Cords

You are connected to everything and everyone around you through invisible energetic chords. These places and people will be part of your life forever. However, there are some relationships that no longer serve you. Your invisible bond will remain intact even when you physically detach yourself from them. Say you broke up with your partner and moved out of the house. If you are hung up on them and can't move on, it's because you are still connected.

Call on Michael; he will cut the energetic chord with his sword and release you from your past relationships.

He Is Always by Your Side

Most people turn to their family and friends whenever they need support. As you grow older, you will realize that people can't always be there for you. This doesn't make them bad friends or family members. They just lead busy lives. Even though they want to be there for you, life can sometimes get in the way.

However, no one is ever really alone. Angels are always around you. Don't be afraid to call on Michael. While everyone in your life is busy, he is always available anytime during the day. In some cases, you won't want anything from Michael. You just need him by your side. Call on him and tell him that you only need to feel his presence to know that everything will be fine eventually.

Symbols Associated with Archangel Michael

Sometimes, Michael will call on you. Perhaps he wants to reach out to you to deliver a message from God, warn you against something, or let you know that he has heard your call and will come to your aid. However, some of the messages he sends aren't straightforward. Each angel has their own symbols that they use to communicate with mankind. Learn Michael's signs so you can instantly tell when he reaches out to you.

The Name Michael

This is one of the easiest signs you can pick up on immediately. If you keep seeing or hearing the name Michael everywhere, this can be the angel trying to tell you something. This will happen through random events that will take place in a short amount of time. You wake up in the morning and check social media, then you see a piece of news about a guy named Michael, but you don't think much of it. While driving to work, you hear a song on the radio by Michel Jackson. You are sitting at the office, and a friend shows you a book she is reading. You accidentally drop it, and it opens on a random page starting with the name Michael. Obviously, these events can't be considered simple coincidences; this is the Archangel trying to get your attention.

Perhaps you are going through a hard time, and Michael wants to let you know he is here for you and everything will work out.

The Color Blue

Archangel Michael is associated with the color blue. It is a common color that you can easily see everywhere. If you keep seeing it more than usual, it is clearly a sign from him. For instance, every day on your way to work, you see four blue cars, you see a blue jay flying by every morning, or you subconsciously wear blue for three days in a row. Pay attention to these messages.

You can also randomly see flashes of blue light when he wants to reach out to you. The light will be very clear and hard to miss since Michael's symbols are rarely subtle.

Feathers

You keep seeing feathers everywhere you go. You find two on your doormat, a friend gives you a necklace with a feather pendant, or you keep seeing large numbers of birds in the sky. This symbol indicates that Michael wants to make you aware of his presence and lets you know he is here for you.

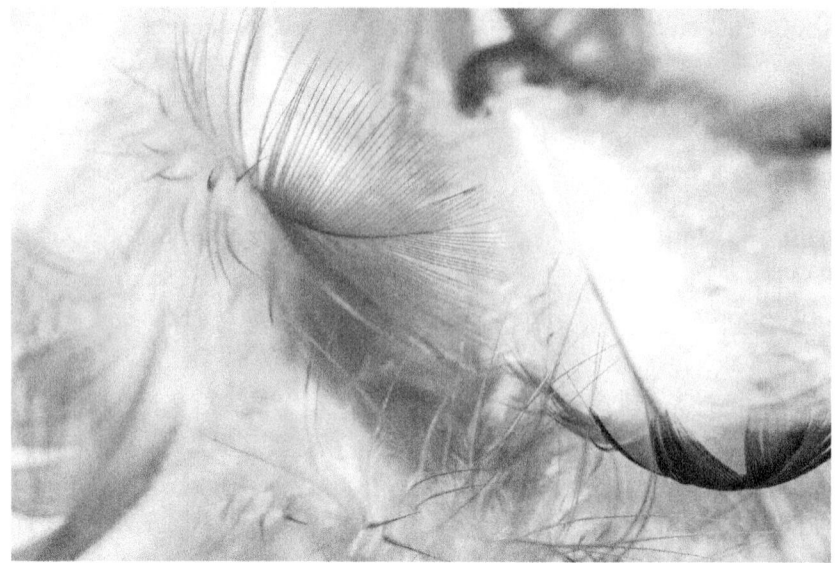

Seeing a feather is a sign from Michael wants you to be aware of his presence.
https://unsplash.com/photos/1YMbHxtntRo

Déjà Vu

Michael will use déjà vu to get your attention when something that can change your life is about to happen.

The Number Eleven

Michael is associated with the number eleven, and he will often use it to try to communicate with you. Your watch could stop at eleven o'clock, or you might keep seeing the number everywhere you look.

Dreams

Michael or other angels can appear to you in your dreams. These dreams will usually be vivid and comforting. Pay attention to every detail, as they could contain hidden messages from Michael.

Voices

As Michael is never subtle with his messages, he can directly speak to you. Say you are about to cross the street and hear a loud voice telling you to stop. You notice a drunk man driving like a maniac could have hit you if you had crossed the street. Sometimes, the voice can be a whisper. Either way, the message should be obvious, so don't ignore it.

He can also send you a message through other people. For instance, you apply for a job and feel that you will get accepted, so you decide to quit your current job. Suddenly, your sister calls you to chat and, out of nowhere, tells you about her co-worker who quit his job after going to a couple of interviews because he thought he believed he would most likely get accepted in one of them. However, he has been unemployed for six months now and regrets his decision. Upon hearing this story, you decide to stay in your job until you hear from the other company. This is clearly a warning from Michael.

Working with archangels can be intimidating, especially with one as powerful as Michael. Angels are created to support and guide mankind, so dare to call on him, and he will always answer the call. Remember, you are never alone. Michael is by your side, providing guidance and assistance whenever you need him, so never despair. He can reach out to you to help or warn you, so pay attention to the world around you to recognize his messages.

Chapter 2: How to Call Upon Archangel Michael

Archangel Michael can be called upon for various reasons. However, before you determine a specific intention, you first need to learn how to make contact with him. In this chapter, you'll learn about the many ways you can call upon Archangel Michael, from mediation and prayers to free writing and dreamwork and using crystals and astral projection. You'll also find instructions for the best ways to contact him for the first time.

Astral Projection

Astral projection involves leaving one's body and journeying to the astral plane. This approach requires very deep meditation and focus (which takes lots of practice), and it can be a great way to get in touch with archangels. Archangel Michael is the closest archangel to divine power. Working with him can empower your spiritual practices and elevate your spirituality. Using astral projection will help you form a deeper connection with this angelic being. With his help, you'll reach a higher level of consciousness, which will make you more susceptible to the angel's messages.

It is recommended to only practice astral projection when you have mastered more profound meditation techniques. This also involves practicing visualization techniques, as astral traveling often requires you to envision scenarios related to your intent. Having learned visualization and meditation, you can reach a deeper level of consciousness. This is almost like a trance-like state, where your spirit can travel freely, gathering knowledge and wisdom from all the different realms.

Free Writing

The written word has a powerful effect on empowering your spiritual work. It can channel your energy and make it flow in the direction of your intention. Besides healing, writing can also help you manifest positive life changes, especially if you use it to summon Archangel Michael to your side. One way to use writing to contact this angel is journaling.

Free writing requires focus and intention to channel the archangel's energy.
https://unsplash.com/photos/y02jEX_B0O0

Sharing your thoughts and needs in a journal is a great way to build a personal relationship with Archangel Michael. Another way to write to Michael is free writing. This requires setting an intention and writing down whatever comes to mind without conscious control. You are channeling his energy, so staying focused will take a lot of practice. Just let the angel guide your hands whenever you feel:

- the need to share your deepest aspirations, trepidations, and feelings with someone
- the desire to make positive changes in your life, but you aren't sure where and how to begin this new chapter

- helpless due to being stuck in the past and that you're constantly focusing on thoughts that are interfering with your present
- a lack of resources and opportunities to fulfill any part of your life or to find your life's purpose
- insecure or afraid of a certain situation, person, or the unknown
- hurt by someone close to you
- the need to express your gratitude for everything you have

After writing with your intention, you can look at it and try to decipher it. Depending on your experience, the message might not make sense to you right away. However, when you're ready, you can acknowledge it and use it to your advantage.

Meditation

Regardless of your reason for meditating with Archangel Michael, he will provide you with the clarity you need to find what you're searching for. For that reason alone, meditation is a great way to channel Michael's energy and summon him to your side. He can help you unclog your mind of stressful thoughts, elevate your spirituality, or even clear out your blocked chakras if needed. Simply reaching out to him during a quick daily meditation can be an elevating experience that will allow you to move forward.

There are several ways to meditate with Michael, with morning meditation being the most common one. In the morning, you feel the most relaxed, and it's easier for you to focus on clearing your mind, center yourself, and manifest your intention. You can combine this with a morning prayer or invocation dedicated to Michael.

One of the other ways is chakra meditation. This involves setting the intention of raising your energies in your chakras and channeling them toward connecting with Michael. The chakras are the main energy points of the body. They are connected to the major organs and all the physical, biological, and spiritual processes transpiring in you. Since summoning Michael requires a heightened level of spiritual energy, it's best to focus on your third eye chakra when meditating with him. Opening this chakra directly influences your ability to soothe your body, silence your mind and enhance your psychic abilities. Your third eye chakra is your best tool for tapping into your higher self and acknowledging the presence of angelic guardians. Once you start practicing chakra meditation, you will find it easier to notice the signs Michael sends back acknowledgment of your newly-established connection.

Positive Affirmations

Just like mantras, positive affirmations enhance the energy of your intention. They also empower your bond with Archangel Michael, even if it's the first time you're reciting them. Besides speaking them out loud, you can also sing them. Remember, angels like music and singing, and Michael is no different. The positive affirmations should be expressed in the present tense and an upbeat tone. Even if something hasn't happened yet, you must believe that it will. The more you do it, the more likely it will happen. For example, you can say:

"I have Archangel Michael's strength by my side, and I know it will help me clear all the hindrances out of my pathway."

Besides empowering you with the knowledge of your strengths, it will also let Michael know that you're thinking about them. He will see this as an invitation to join you on your life journey.

Chanting

Sometimes all you need to do to connect with Archangel Michael is chant his name. Suppose you suddenly find yourself in a tough situation and need urgent help. In that case, you can simply say Michael's name out loud several times. He will listen to you and respond even if you don't notice his response immediately (whether you do or not depends on your experience with spiritual communication and ability to tap into your intuition). Or, you can chant his name to acknowledge your belief that Michael will help you whether you ask for his assistance or not.

Mantras

A mantra is a way to channel your energy into your words. Your words carry unique vibrations. Coupled with an energetic intention, the spoken word can become a powerful tool for delivering vibrations and messages to the universe. Remember, everything has energy, and this energy is alive. You can consciously channel your energy to connect with the energy around you, including angelic essences. You have the extraordinary power to link your energy to thoughts, emotions, and actions and influence the outcomes of your energetic exchanges. You can use the vibrations of your mantras to call on Archangel Michael's energetic force and use it for what you want. For starters, you'll need mantras that help you establish a profound connection with this angel. However, this will require practice, and you'll need to be patient because don't happen overnight.

Looking at Images

Some people find it useful to look at pictures or other representations of Michael to establish a connection with him. Gazing intently at Michael's likeness can send a powerful message to the angel. It also helps you tap into your higher self. Practicing this method is a way of affirming your connection with Michael without spending too much energy. It's a great strategy for beginners who wish to connect with Archangel Michael.

Using Representations of Michael

You can use items associated with Archangel Michael to summon him. You can place these in your sacred space (altar or shrine) or wherever you need his help the most. You can also carry them with you for added reassurance and protection. For example, you can light a blue candle and place it on your altar. Blue is the color associated with Michael, and his energy is often envisioned as an orb of blue light. You can say a prayer, mantra, or invocation when lighting the candle, or make this step part of your meditation with the angel. Wearing blue clothes when using any method for summoning the angel is also a powerful way to channel them and your intention to establish a connection with them.

Carrying objects representing Archangel Michael is a subtle way of anchoring the angel to you. It channels his energy (and his attention) to you, so you'll always feel protected by him. Tap into your intuition and choose an item that feels right for you. It could be a feather, a coin, or whatever object you feel drawn to when thinking of Michael. It can also be a crystal associated with the angel. Opt for blue or clear stones with high vibrational frequencies. The higher the crystal vibrates, the easier it will be to channel its energy to your intention. Angelite, blue chalcedony, lapis lazuli, and clear quartz are all great choices. Dedicate the chosen item to the angel by saying an affirmation or mantra reassuring you of Michael's presence and willingness to assist you.

Prayer

While many pray to Archangel Michael in times of need, you can also use this method to summon him just to get to know him better or thank him for his blessing and presence. Prayer is an incredibly powerful way to channel spiritual energy, regardless of your religious preferences. Prayer is empowering, opens one's mind, and deters errant thoughts that could hinder one's intention. Simply knowing and believing that Michael is there to hear your prayers can give you emotional resilience and enable you to overcome any obstacle in life. You don't have to face challenges. You just have to have an open heart to accept Michael's presence, and prayer is a great way to reinforce this knowledge. Through prayer, you can let him know that you appreciate him, which allows him to step into your life. It's like talking to someone who is always there for you when you need them to support you, offer advice, or simply listen.

Calling Out to Archangel Michael

The simplest way to connect with Archangel Michael is to call on him and ask him to join you. You can ask him to accompany you wherever you are or invite him to join you at work or at an event where you might need a little boost. You don't have to ask him for a specific favor, just ask him to join you, and he will come. You can do this when you feel like there's too much negativity around you or when you feel ready to get to know the angel. This method doesn't require much preparation or practice. It can also help you hone your intuition. After making your plea, you'll need to listen to the signs telling you that he has accepted your invitation. Sooner or later, his presence will be known, and it's up to you to learn how to deepen your connection with him.

Inviting Archangel Michael into Your Dreams

Some people find it easier to communicate with supernatural beings through dreams. While angels have no limitations for spiritual communication, people do. Dreams can provide a safe medium for spiritual messages if you aren't sure how to communicate safely in your waking life. So, if you're ready to connect with the angel, invite him to join you in your dreams. You can do this by praying to him, lighting a candle, or doing a quick meditation with him before going to bed. Your subconscious will help you put aside the stress and enable you to interpret angelic messages. You can combine dream work with journaling and record the messages that you receive in your dreams. This way, you'll be able to revisit them and decipher those that didn't make sense at first. You can even ask Archangel Michael questions about himself to learn how he likes communicating and his preferences regarding contact and summoning. Remember that you might not receive answers to all your questions right away. However, they will come eventually, so keep an eye out for them!

Practical Techniques for Connecting with Archangel Michael

Here are several easy strategies for summoning this angel and asking him to join your side:

Archangel Michael Morning Invocation

You can invoke Archangel Michael first thing in the morning if you think you'll have a rough day. He can guide you through the day's challenges, and the two of you can learn more about each other. Here is an invocation you can use to summon Michael:

> *"I call on you, oh powerful Archangel Michael,*
> *Who was sent by the universe to be by my side.*
> *I ask you with all my heart and power,*
> *For you to bless me with your presence on this day.*
> *Hold my hand and guide me,*
> *May your presence bless my day with strength and courage.*
> *Archangel Michael, surround me now with blessed energy*
> *And remain by the side of your faithful follower*
> *Who I will become now that our connection has been made."*

Archangel Michael Meditation

The following meditation will help you make an initial connection with Archangel Michael. You can combine meditative practice with prayers, invocations, or any other way that helps build a powerful bond with this angel.

Instructions:

1. Find a quiet place where you can focus on calling upon Michael. Sit in a chair or with your back to the wall. The goal is to relax your shoulders, all while avoiding slouching or tensing up.
2. Take a few deep breaths to center yourself and start grounding. Visualize your legs taking root, tying you to the ground. You should feel them pulling you towards the earth as your spiritual grounding nears completion.
3. When you feel rooted and secure, you can move on to the next step, visualizing Archangel Michael. If it helps, close your eyes. Conjure up an image of the angel standing in front of you,

surrounded by bright blue light.
4. See his flaming sword, the symbol of his protection, and allow yourself to be reassured by his presence. When you're ready, call out to the angel.
5. You can say whatever comes to mind, greet him, ask him questions, or do anything else you want. Avoid asking favors. The purpose of this exercise is to establish a connection.

Archangel Michael Prayers

The following two prayers are used to call upon Michael. Use the first prayer right after waking up to reestablish and strengthen your connection with him. The other one is an evening prayer you recite when winding down for the day. It can help you express gratitude or ask for signs for the following day.

Morning Prayer:

"May the mighty Archangel Michael be sent to my side,

To guide me, blessing me with his presence.

I am willing to put my faith and trust in you, Michael,

As I know that you can provide me with the strength and courage I need.

May our connection be as bright as your sword light,

To clear all blocks and obstacles that stand in our way."

Evening Prayer:

"I offer my gratitude for your divine guidance Archangel Michael

I have felt your presence today.

I have sensed your strength, trust, and faith in me.

I thank you, Michael, for being by my side."

Walking with Archangel Michael

Walking with Michael is a great way to communicate with him. It's a form of active meditation and involves the same essential elements as regular meditation – finding focus and channeling your mind toward your intention.

Instructions:

1. Walk briskly for ten minutes in a place where you can focus your mind – nature is the best place. Slow to a regular walking

pace and continue for about two minutes.

2. Then, think about your intention of talking with Archangel Michael. Send him thoughts of gratitude and love and desire to meet him.

3. Now, envision Michael walking beside you. Thank him for joining you, and tell him whatever comes to mind. Don't ask for favors, and only talk about you or him.

4. Listen to whatever he has to say in response, and thank him for his answer.

5. If you have trouble envisioning him beside you, don't worry. You can still talk to him. He will hear you even if you can't see him just yet.

6. Whatever the outcome, just enjoy your walk. Even if Archangel Michael doesn't appear, he will send you messages sooner or later.

Mantra Repetition

When repeating mantras, it is crucial to do so while focusing on your intention. Since mantras work best when they're personal, try to write your own angel-invoking mantra. That said, here is how to get the best out of using mantras for calling on Archangel Michael.

1. Set the intention. Think about what you want to accomplish. Do you want Michael to contact you in a specific way? Maybe you want to summon him to learn more about him.

2. Whatever you need the angelic mantra for, keep it in mind. You can do this by bringing up an emotion that thinking of the intentions provokes in you. Once you determine the emotions, you'll know which mantra to choose.

3. Go to your sacred space. This can be any space you dedicate for spiritual practice. You can create an altar or shrine or use one regular spot where you feel safe and focused, from your bathroom to a tranquil patch of nature.

4. Settle into a comfortable position, breathe deeply, and allow yourself to relax. When your breath slows down and deepens, your body will release tension, and your mind will stop racing. You will then enter into a light meditative state.

5. Inhale and exhale 5-6 times to fully direct your focus to your intention. With each breath, you will channel more and more

energy into your intent until you reach an absolute taste of calmness and concentration.

6. Now, envision an orb of blue light in front of you. Watch it grow until you see Archangel Michael emerge from it. Think about your desire to connect with him, and he will help you make the connection by extending his energy toward you.

7. Once you sense his energy surrounding you, you will feel a sense of lightness. You can now start chanting your mantra to further empower your bond with the angel. Say it out loud or silently in your mind.

8. After three to five minutes of mantra repetition, you'll see Archangel Michael smiling at you, reassuring you of his presence and protection. You can let the image go and slowly emerge from the meditative state.

9. Repeat the mantras frequently. The more you do so, the stronger your bond with the angel will become. He will be more sensitive to your needs, and you'll find it easier to call on him.

Chapter 3: Signs That Archangel Michael Is Present

This chapter offers a list of signs that Archangel Michael has answered your call. These signs can include seeing feathers or angel numbers, seeing the color blue often, and many others. You'll also find a few personal stories of people who have successfully connected to or "seen" Archangel Michael.

The Most Common Signs of Archangel Michael's Presence

Physical Signs

Physical signs are the most common ways that Archangel Michael will communicate with you. They can also be coupled with other signs that make you feel that the angel is present. Michael likes to take a straightforward approach and leave you an unmistakable sign of his presence. Some signs will be more subtle than others, but if you have already reached out to Michael, you'll only have to rely on your intuition to decipher them. In any case, if you notice one of the following things standing out in some way in your environment, you can be sure that the angel is present:

- **Feathers** – These are the universal calling cards of angels. If you keep finding feathers around you, you'll know that the Archangel is near.

- **Butterflies** - They are a signal of reassurance of Michael's presence.
- **White birds** - Another group of winged creatures that often act as messages to angels. Archangel Michael could be sending them to you to help you feel his love and bring peace to you.
- **Breadcrumbs** - Leaving a trail of breadcrumbs is the angel's way of letting you know you can rely on divine powers.
- **Temperature** - An unmistakable sign of a powerful angel being present is the sudden drop in temperature. This is often followed by an instant feeling of warmth emanating from Michael.

Orbs of Light

If you've called upon Archangel Michael before, you already have his protection. To reassure you of this, he will send you messages in the form of colorful sparks, flashes of blue light, and orbs. If you haven't welcomed him yet and he feels that you're in need of protection or healing, sending you those things can be his way of asking you to let him in. You might see a long streak of light or an orb floating in front of you for a couple of minutes. Or, you might see a flash of light out of nowhere when you're just going about your day. Either way, seeing his light will make you feel warm and loved. You'll know that you're surrounded by Michael's protection, and you will be relying on his guidance from then on.

Seeing orbs or sparks of light indicates that Michael is asking to be let in.
https://unsplash.com/photos/M-xaOaCzv_M

Tones of Blue and Purple

Noticing tones of blue and purple can also indicate Archangel Michael's presence. As a powerful Archangel, Michael is associated with colored light, unlike other, lesser angels whose light is white. This relates to his divine purpose, which is protection. The colors purple and blue are linked to the protective layer of the aura of all living beings. They are also associated with Michael's most well-known qualities, serenity, determination, honesty, and truth. If you suddenly notice these colors pop up around you, you can be certain that Michael is present.

A Warm, Tingling Sensation

There are several reasons you might feel warm or tingly if Michael is present. He has a very powerful essence, and his bold protective instinct is transmitted on higher frequencies. When these frequencies reach you, you'll feel the warmth of his protectiveness wash over you. As a result, you'll feel satisfied and happy. Second, Michael is the Archangel associated with the Sun. He is even depicted with a flaming sword at times. So, if you feel a sudden wave of heat coupled with a positive energy flow, it's a sign that Michael is there to boost your mood and spirits.

Images of Swords, Warriors, or Archangel Michael

If you keep seeing pictures of warriors, swords, or Michael himself, this could also be the angel's way of making his presence known. You might see him in paintings, statues, and other art forms. Some of these might be accompanied by words such as evil and slaying. Swords and warriors are among his correspondences, so these are his signs too. For example, you might see paintings of warriors battling evil. Or, you might encounter this motive in a video game. If any of these appear for no apparent reason, pay attention to them because they might be messages from Archangel Michael.

A Feeling of Uplifting or Grounding Energy

Archangel Michael provides the perfect balance of energies that will uplift you and ground you at the same time. If you feel a sense of security and spiritual improvement, the angel signals that you won't have to worry about having enough strength to overcome your obstacles. It might feel like being wrapped in a protective blanket that also provides resilience and endurance. Or, you might suddenly realize that you can overcome the challenge you're currently facing or about to face. You might also have a sudden moment of clarity, feeling grounded, and having a renewed sense of focus. Either way, you won't miss this energy for sure.

A Sense of Peace

Having an overwhelming sense of peace could also denote the angel's presence. Being a great protector, Michael will offer a comforting presence. Regardless of your situation, you'll feel at peace and sure that everything will turn out all right. This is because having this angel near you wards off negative energies and harmful influences. It's like being embraced by invisible wings. If the sense of peace is also accompanied by love and a surge of positivity that calms your worries and uplifts your hearts, know that Archangel Michael is there to reassure you of his presence, listen to you, and even dry your tears if necessary.

The Name "Michael"

Besides his image, Michael's name can appear as a sign of him being around. If you keep encountering the name Michael wherever you go without any reason for it (it's not your name or any of your loved ones'), this might be the Archangel letting you know that he is by your side. For example, you might encounter several people named Michal (a cashier, a server at a restaurant, a co-worker, etc.), hear or see it in the news, or when browsing the internet. Typically, you'll run into his name several times in one day. The specific ways the name appears might offer clues on what message the angel is trying to send. For example, hearing it in the news could be a warning sign. While running into a co-worker named Michael could be a hint to pay more attention to your work.

Feeling Safe and Protected

Sometimes, the only sign you'll receive from Michael is a feeling of safety. This can come independently of your spiritual work and might even take you by surprise. You just suddenly feel protected and safe for no reason. You don't know why, but you feel nothing can hurt you at the moment. Michael's powerful protective energy will surprise you even if you've requested protection or taken measures to protect yourself from harmful influences. It will give you a sense of direction, and you'll intuitively know how to raise your protective energies. Acknowledging that the feeling of safety means Michael's presence will fill you with confidence for moving forward in life and your ability to manifest the changes you want. You know that nothing will deter you from your goal, no matter how scary the obstacles seemed a couple of minutes ago. Your fear has now diminished because you know he is there with you.

Trust Your Intuition

If this is your first time working with an angel, you're probably still learning to listen to your intuition (especially when receiving and deciphering angelic messages). However, after contacting Michael, you might notice that you can trust your gut feelings more. The presence of Archangel Michael causes a powerful energetic shift around you, raising your vibrations. While this energy is different, and you can't explain why it is, you just know you can trust it.

Hearing Michael's Voice

Another direct way Michael announces his presence is by speaking to you directly. If you've invited him into your life and started hearing a voice that is different from your inner one, that is probably the Archangel's. This is particularly common with beginners who find it easier to receive messages in a more mundane way. The angel lets you know he is there and ready to listen to you by whispering in your ear. Wondering how you can tell that what you hear is his voice and not that of your inner monologue? It's simple. You'll know because it will be much stronger. Some report it is a booming sound that states a message loud and clear. Unlike other angels who send subtle messages through music and other sounds, Archangel Michael will get straight to the point. If you suddenly hear a blunt warning not to proceed with something, listen to it. Michael is warning you that the action can have serious negative consequences and lead you down a path you don't want to go. If you hear a calm voice offering advice, he simply tries to guide you in the right direction. Regardless of how you hear Archangel Michael, know that his message always comes from a place of love. Those with heightened physical abilities like clairaudience will be more susceptible to auditory messages from Michael. Conversely, those with claircognizance will simply know that the voice they hear comes from this angel.

Persistence

Have you lacked determination in the past but now feel the urge to remain persistent in working toward your goals? If you are determined to persist - regardless of how challenging the road might seem - Michael is probably guiding you. Persistence is one of his most admirable traits.

The Urge to Defend

When you come under Archangel Michael's influence, you might feel the need to defend someone from injustice. Let's say you hear that your co-worker is about to be punished for someone else's mistake. Instead of letting it go (because you fear you'll be disciplined, too), you stand up and voice your outrage in the face of that injustice. Archangel Michael has a protective streak a mile long. By passing on some of his qualities, he shows you how you can connect with him. Likewise, you might also have the need to confront your adversaries. This could be something as simple as finally letting the neighbor know that you're not okay with them listening to loud music in the middle of the night. Or, you simply decide to control your biggest deterrents – your own fears. Whether it's fear of a specific situation or the unknown, you'll suddenly be encouraged to take risks and see where things go. By facing your fears, you might encounter new opportunities or learn that you have nothing to fear at all.

A Pull toward Archangel Michael

If you've invited Archangel Michael into your life, you might need to start working with him immediately. If this is the case, this indicates that he has received your call and is ready to build a connection with you. Whether you want to request healing, get a spiritual reading with him, or work with him in any other way that contributes to your spiritual fulfillment, he is willing to participate. Archangel Michael has the power to channel energies and intentions, which ultimately pushes you in the right direction. While he won't force you to do anything (he is a fan of free will), he can help you make better choices. One of his ways of doing this is by making you feel like you're pulled toward a certain type of spiritual work that he can help you explore. This thought might pop up when you tap into your gut feelings. If you've just made the first call to him and haven't asked him for his assistance, he might be telling you that you should. Maybe he is trying to tell you that to work with him, you need to heal from an emotional trauma first, and he is offering to accompany you on this healing journey. If you don't understand why you are feeling an intense pull toward Archangel Michael, look at the bigger picture. Look for other signs as well and ask for more if needed. Asking Michael questions is the best way to build a connection with him, particularly if you feel drawn to him.

Finding Your Life's Purpose

If you've been struggling to find your life's purpose and you've suddenly encountered it recently, you can be sure that it had something to do with Archangel Michael. Michael motivates you to become more productive, so you can have a fulfilled life and attain spiritual enlightenment. He is there to let you know he will help you develop your talents and skills to fulfill your purpose. Whether you've found something that benefits you and your loved ones or your entire community, Michael will certainly support you in your endeavors. He will help you remain determined, organized, and stick to the routine that keeps you in the proper rhythm as you work towards your goals. You can verify this by reaching out to Archangel Michael after you've made the first steps toward fulfilling your life's purpose.

Keeping Relationships Simple

If you have struggled with constant conflicts in one or more of your relationships, Michael can send you a message that will help you resolve the issue. For example, you might receive a message in your dreams or the morning after a fight with your partner before going to bed. Or, you might see a sudden flash of blue light as you're arguing with your employer while demanding a raise. If any of these scenarios are repeated more than once, it can indicate that Archangel Michael wants to guide you in the right direction. He wants you to resolve the conflicts that are complicating your relationships. He knows relationships are only fulfilling when based on simple yet profound emotions, ideas, and values.

Testimonies of People Who Recognized Archangel Michael's Signs

Countless records of people encountering or verifying their successful connection with Archangel Michael exist. Below are some of them.

"One morning, I woke up and walked out onto my balcony to get some fresh air while having my first cup of coffee of the day. It was a late spring morning with clear skies, and I was still sleepy. Standing with my cup in my hand, I suddenly noticed something floating in the air in front of me. As it got closer, I realized it was a white feather. When it reached the height of my face, it stopped and just hovered in front of my eyes for a few seconds and then was carried away by a slight breeze. At first, I didn't know where the feather came from because there were no birds in the sky. And even stranger was the way it lingered in front of me. Then I remembered reaching out to Archangel Michael several days before, asking for a sign that he was ready to work

with me. I realized the feather was Michael telling me he was here with me now. When the feather kept appearing in other places, too, I knew I'd interpreted the sign correctly." - Olivia

"I was haunted by a disturbing, heavy presence for several days, and I didn't know where it came from. I didn't think anyone near me would wish me ill will, but I was wrong. Wanting to learn the origin of this negative energy in my life, I asked for Archangel Michael's help. I lit a candle and prayed to him, asking him to send me a sign before going to bed. Michael came into my dreams and let me know it was my best friend poisoning me with his toxic energies. He was envious of my accomplishments and wanted me to fail. Michael came to warn me of him and asked me to pray for my friend. Suddenly, the negative presence no longer controlled me. I will forever be thankful to Michael for pointing this out." - Charlie

"I've struggled with depression most of my life. After losing my mother, I felt so lost. I wanted to be by myself and refused to leave home. I knew this wasn't good for me, so I decided to ask Archangel Michael to help me heal. I have always liked meditation, so I thought this could be the best way to start my healing journey. After praying to Michael, I relaxed my mind and summoned him to my side. Suddenly, I saw a bright blue orb in front of me. At first, I felt scared, but then I heard Michael telling me not to be afraid. The light got closer and eventually enveloped me before connecting with me. I felt as if it started draining negativity from me. When there was no negativity left, the light vanished. I thanked Michael for his help and reemerged from my meditative state. I felt much lighter and knew that I could be happy. From then on, I decided to regularly work with Archangel Michael. Soon after, I started feeling better, and slowly, the smile returned to my face." - Laura

Chapter 4: Requesting Protection

Archangel Michael is a spiritual warrior and leader of the army of angels. He fights against evil, which makes him perfect for guarding against harmful influences. Who better to call upon when you need protection? In this chapter, you'll find several ways to acquire the Archangel's protective shield, including prayers, meditations, amulets, and more.

Archangel Michael is a spiritual warrior.
https://pixabay.com/es/photos/miguel-san-miguel-arc%C3%A1ngel-5764009/

Protection Charm Infused with Michael's Powers

Carrying a charm or talisman infused with Archangel Michael's powers will always make you feel protected. Whenever you feel that you're in danger, the charm will be there as a reminder of Michael's love and protection. It works best if you first cleanse your body and space of harmful energies.

Ingredients:
- A white candle
- A piece of red fabric – large enough for your talisman
- Bay leaf
- Vinegar
- Dried chili pepper
- Coarse sea salt
- Essential oil associated with Michael
- An image or symbol of Archangel Michael
- A needle
- Red thread
- Scissors
- Safety pin (optional)

Instructions:
1. Take the sea salt into your hands and start walking clockwise. Sprinkle the salt around, making a circle large enough to sit in.
2. Anoint the candle with the essential oil, and light it while calling upon Archangel Michael.
3. Using the needle and thread, make a pouch from the fabric. Put the chili pepper, bay leaf, the representation of Michael, and a pinch of salt inside it, dip the needle into the vinegar, and sew the pouch shut.
4. Imagine a beam of blue light shining down on you, enveloping your body, until it starts radiating too.
5. Then recite the following: *"May this holy flame burn above me, May this holy flame burn below me, May this holy flame burn*

beside me, May this holy flame burn in front of me, May this holy flame burn behind me, May this whole female burn be within me, My Michael will always be with me."

6. Snuff out the candle. You can light it again when you wish to invoke Michael's protection again.
7. Secure the pouch inside your clothes or bag with the safety pin if you prefer. If not, just place it there where you need its protective powers.
8. To reinforce the power of Michael's protective fire, take some sea salt and sprinkle it around the entrances of your home, including window sills and back doors.

A Ritual to Call on Archangel Michael for Protection

With the following ritual, you can request Michael's protection and ask him to remove negative energy. Traditionally, this ritual would be performed on a day associated with Archangel Michael. However, you can do it any day you prefer. Before the ritual, cleanse yourself both spiritually and mentally.

Ingredients:
- Tools for cleansing your space and items
- Tools for purifying your body
- A red candle
- Michael-associated oil to amount the candle
- A talisman charged with Michael's protective powers

Instructions:

1. Declutter your space and clean it. Then, light an incense or smudge stick to cleanse it spiritually. Alternatively, you can anoint the entrances with essential oil or sprinkle salt mixed with herbs associated with Archangel Michael.
2. Cleanse your body with a salt bath, and purify your tools with salt, smoke, or any other method you prefer.
3. When you're ready, find a comfortable position, take a deep breath, and focus on invoking Archangel Michael. Chant the following:

> *"I call upon your power Archangel Michael*
> *I acknowledge your strength and courage*
> *And I offer my gratitude for your presence in my life.*
> *As you've dominated evil,*
> *I ask you to help me overpower what threatens me*
> *Protect me, my space, and my loved ones from evil influences.*
> *Guard me against anything that can harm me*
> *Anyone who wishes me ill will.*
> *I thank you again, Michael."*

4. Light the red candle and place it in a safe place. Let it burn down completely, but snuff it out anytime you can't attend to it.
5. When the candle has burned down, bury the remaining wax in the ground. You can do this in your garden, a pot on your windowsill, or in the park.
6. Take the talisman and place it where you need the most protection. If it's your home, put it in your entryway. If it's for you, carry it with you.

A Prayer to Archangel Michael

Praying to Archangel Michael is the most straightforward and surefire way to obtain his protection. It can be used for any occasion and combined with invocations, meditations, or any other strategies you might want to use to petition for Michael's protection.

Instructions:
1. Sit in front of your sacred space. This could be an altar or any place where you feel safe and focused.
2. If you wish, light a candle in the name of Michael. Then, recite the following prayer:

> *"I pray to you, Michael, the heavenly prince who defends us in battle,*
> *Whether it's between the powers of darkness and light,*
> *Or the battle of spiritual principalities.*
> *I ask you to come to my aid now,*
> *And join a fellow creation made to the creator's likeness.*

Help me redeem myself from influences I couldn't ward off,
And fight the battles of the spirit alongside your angels.
I know dark energies are powerless to resist your omnipotent essence,
On the Earth and every other realm in the universe.
You are the slayer of the enemy,
Who transformed into a being of light.
And as you wander among the wicked spirit,
Slay them all, casting them out of the universe.
I ask you to protect me against these impure forces,
Which threaten to deprive my mind and corrupt my heart.
Help me remain free of these energies,
And avoid falling into the trap of lies, resentment, and fear.
I know my obstacles and enemies can be formidable,
But with your help, I can overcome even the craftiest of challenges.
Help set a light of protection around me,
And use your sword to ward away anything that threatens me."

3. Repeat the prayer three times in a row. Only stop to take a deep breath between each repetition.
4. Once you're finished with the prayer, you can state a petition if you have one. If you do, be as specific as you can. For example, if you feel threatened by a specific person, ask Michael to protect you from them.
5. Alternatively, you can meditate for a couple of minutes after your prayer or simply go about your day or night. When you're finished, snuff out the candle.

Visualizing Michael's Shield

This visualization meditation will help you invite Michael's protection into your life. It will help you feel safe and protected as you work on expressing your authentic self. It makes you confident in embracing your light and leaving behind any interference that comes from the external or internal environment.

Instructions:
1. Find a secluded space where you can focus without any distractions. Get comfortable by relaxing your body and mind.
2. Focus on deepening your breathing, and imagine breathing in light energy. Feel how the light enters your body. At the same time, with each exhalation, you release any energy that doesn't belong to you.
3. Once your entire body (all dimensions, physical, mental, and spiritual) is filled with light, you can call on your spiritual helpers. Start with your higher self, as this is where your power lies, and this is what will help you attract and use Michael's shield.
4. Then, ask Archangel Michael and all angels working with him to join you. Close your eyes and visualize Michael's sword floating in front of you, enveloped in an electric blue flame.
5. Feel how the sword's flame is reaching you, permeating your body, and clearing out all layers of your body, first the physical, then the metaphysical (the chakras and aura layers).
6. Then, feel how the flame reaches your emotions, clearing any negative or confusing feelings and emotions that you have picked up from others. Along with the emotions, the flame will eliminate all energies that don't belong to you but are clouding your emotional judgment.
7. Other people's ideas, thoughts, beliefs, and judgments are now released from your mind. Your energies are disentangled from the negative ones threatening it.
8. Now, ask Michael to help you seal your freshly cleansed energy. Visualize the electric blue field surrounding your body.
9. As the light seals your body, imagine yourself reaching out to the sword, placing it in front of your heart to seal your heart chakra. Next, move the sword towards your back, sealing yourself from that side as well.
10. After your front and back, seal your left and right side, then move the sword above your head before going to your feet, protecting the above and beyond space.
11. Imagine being protected by seven swords, one from each direction you sealed your energies and one from within. Take a

deep breath and tap into your higher self. Feel how you are empowered by higher frequency energies while the lower ones are unable to enter your energy field.

12. Breathe and allow the alignment of protection to create a shield around you. This is Michael's, and you can call on it anytime you need protection. Whenever you need protection, you just have to imagine it multiplying itself, effectively protecting you from all lower-frequency energies.
13. Let all the images go, and keep breathing deeply for a few minutes. During this time, Michael and the angels working with him will intensify the energy of your protective shield.
14. Emerge from your meditation and go about your day, carrying Michael's shield with you wherever you go.

Archangel Michael Chakra Meditation

With this meditation, you can summon Archangel Michael's powerful energy to protect you from spiritual interference. During this exercise, you'll encounter Michael, who will help you cut unhealthy attachments, allowing you to establish a higher connection with your higher self and the spiritual realm of healing, relaxation, and protection.

Instructions:

1. Find a comfortable and quiet space. If you can, do this outside. If you're meditating inside, leave a window open.
2. Close your eyes and focus on your breathing. Feel how the fresh air enters your body and the stale, warm air leaves it. Continue until you feel relaxed enough to connect to your spiritual self.
3. You'll know you're relaxed when you feel you can let go of any thoughts that pop into your head.
4. Now imagine a beam of light coming from the ceiling, reaching the top of your head, and opening your crown chakra. See how your crown chakra opens up like a beautiful purple flower.
5. As the flower opens, it lets the energies in, and you can see it connecting to the divine spirituality, opening the chakra even more. The light then travels down, cleansing your head, relaxing your muscles, and opening your other chakras.

6. When the light reaches your feet, it continues down to earth, rooting you to the ground. Deep inside, you know that the elevated part of you is now open to receive higher energies.

7. You're now connected to both your physical nature and spiritual truth. As you breathe, visualize being surrounded by a beam of blue light. With each breath you take, the light brightens, and you feel blissfully one with the defender of the spiritual realm, Archangel Michael.

8. Feel Michael's energy floating everywhere around you, flooding your chakras. Imagine him walking towards you, with his hair floating around and his sword by his side.

9. As you're admiring Michael's sword, you see Michael opening his wings, making you feel his protective energy. You feel safe, at home, and incredibly thankful for his presence in your life at that present moment.

10. Look at the field of energy around you. You might see lighter and darker aspects; the latter is what you need protection from. As Michael's power draws the darker aspects front, you know he will protect you from them.

11. Next, Michael takes his sword with both hands and cuts any unwanted ties that threaten your spirit. As the ties are cut, you feel a warm and tingling sensation.

12. After that, repeat the following:

    "From now on, I will be protected from harmful energies.
    Only good energy will be allowed into my auric field.
    I ask you, Michael, that with your sword, shield me from
    Anything that's not attached to me through life and light."

13. See how Michael lifts his sword again, blessing you with it. Breathe out and see Michael looking at you with his eyes full of kindness.

14. You now feel that Michael will always watch over you no matter what. Because of this, you'll be as powerful a warrior as possible. Thank Michael for his blessing. Let the images go, and return your focus to your breathing. You feel lighter, stronger, and cleaner as you open your eyes and breathe deeply.

15. Anytime you need a boost, remember that Michael is there. You can use his protection to fight your battles or help others fight theirs; the choice is yours.

Protective Meditation with Archangel Michael

Here is another mediation for calling upon Archangel Michael's protective powers. This is simple and quick. You can do it even if you only have 10 minutes.

Instructions:

1. After finding a secluded spot, start focusing on your breath. As you do so, imagine letting everything go when you exhale.
2. Release every thought and just focus on the moment. Notice how your breath becomes lighter and set your intention to feel safe and protected.
3. As you continue breathing, feel yourself reaching deeper inside until you feel anchored to your higher self, your soul, and all its desires.
4. Now, call on Archangel Michael, asking for his assistance. Invite him from the highest of the realms to join you.
5. Feel free to imagine his presence as you feel comfortable. This might be a human figure or a blue orb of light floating in front of you.
6. As he arrives, you suddenly feel all the negativity around you leave your presence. With the Archangel by your side, you feel loved and protected.
7. Ask Michael to keep you safe and allow this feeling of safety and security you now feel to accompany you. Ask him to protect you everywhere you go.
8. Archangel Michael will heed your request, granting you a protective shield. This shield will prevent anyone from taking something you aren't willing to give.
9. Basking in Michael's security, protection, and love, enjoy feeling safe in this space and that nothing will affect you. Michael will always be by your side.
10. Thank him for bringing you the feeling of safety and love. Finish your meditation by returning to your physical presence.

Whenever you need to feel safe, ask Michael to step in and remind you that you're safe.

Lighting a Candle for Archangel Michael

Lighting candles for Archangel Michael is another fantastic way of letting him know you need his protection. You can do this before a ritual, prayer, meditation, or any other form of spiritual work. For example, you can light a candle before asking Michael to send you a sign in your dreams. This way, you will be protected while communicating with him. You can use any color you want. However, blue candles are the best for channeling his protective powers. Whereas red ones are best for protection against negative influences during spiritual work.

Blue candles are the best to use to ask for his protection.
https://unsplash.com/photos/HK1BuoReZmM

Instructions:

1. Before lighting your candle, cleanse it by rubbing it between your hands or in a bowl of salt. This will remove any negative energy it could've picked up before reaching your hands.

2. As you're cleansing the candle, visualize a black or gray light leaving it. As the candle is freed from negative vibes, it becomes lighter in your hand.

3. Now, focus on your intention and channel it towards the candle. While you do this, rub the candle from the ends toward the middle. At this point, you can also use anointing oils (incorporating oils associated with Michael).

4. When infused with your intention, the candle will slowly release your desire as it burns, helping you manifest it. The candle becomes heavier again.

5. Light the candle and say a prayer to Michael. You can also recite a mantra or simply chant Archangel Michael's name nine times. Then ask Michael for his protection.

6. Let the candle burn down completely. However, don't leave it unattended, and always keep it in an area where you can keep an eye on it. Alternatively, you can place it in a dish with a little water at the bottom. This will catch any sparks that might fly. The intensity of the negative power you need protection from depends on whether there are sparks.

7. Whenever you need to leave the candle unattended, snuff it out. Avoid blowing it because this is considered insulting to Archangel Michael. If you need substantial protection, relight the candle each day and repeat the same ritual/prayer/mantra every time. If not, just light it each day until it burns out.

8. When the candle burns out, look at its remains. If they contain dark soot, that means it has trapped negativity, and you won't need to worry about being affected by it anymore.

9. To avoid having to fight off negativity again, don't touch the candle with your hands. Dispose of the wax to make your defenses whole and allow Michael's protection to envelop you.

10. You should now feel protected. If you don't, light another candle, repeat everything, and ask for Archangel Michael's protection.

Chapter 5: Requesting Healing

Amongst other things, Archangel Michael is often associated with healing. As an Archangel, his energies vibrate at higher frequencies, which gives them powerful restorative effects. Their light is healing, and by connecting to it and harnessing it, you can empower your mind, body, and soul and encourage their healing from traumatic events. Some of the methods you'll be introduced to here include meditating with Archangel Michael's light to heal your energy and physical body, blessing water with Michael's energy, and using his symbols for Reiki and other self-healing methods.

The reiki symbol for Archangel Michael.

Creating Blessed Water with the Energy of Archangel Michael

As he is often associated with water, Archangel Michael can bless the water with his restorative and protective energy. You can use this water to protect yourself from mental, physical, and spiritual influences threatening your health and wellbeing. Here is a great way to ask Michael to bless your water with his energy.

Ingredients:
- 1 cup of spring water
- 1 tablespoons of sea salt
- A bowl
- A jar with a lid

Instructions:
1. Mix all the ingredients in a bowl, and pour them into the jar.
2. Hold the jar up to your chest in front of your heart.
3. Ask Michael to bless the water and infuse it with his divine energy. While you do that, recite the following Prayer to Archangel Michael:

   "Archangel Michael, as you stand before me

   I trust you to protect me wherever I go.

   I ask you to bless this water,

   So, I can use its power to heal myself and my loved ones.

   In the name of the highest good, I ask you now for your blessings.

   Thank you, and I'm looking forward to working with you."

4. Feel how Michael's light empowers the water with love and protection.
5. Sprinkle the water on your body as needed for physical healing. You can also spritz it around you and your space for mental, mental, and spiritual healing.

Using Archangel Michael's Symbol for Reiki and Self-Healing

Archangel Michael's guidance extends beyond infusing with healing light. By building a close relationship with him, you can harness his energy and empower yourself for self-healing. One of the most effective self-healing methods is Reiki, a form of spiritual empowerment in which the person receives restorative energy. This energy unblocks and balances the chakra system and aids in the restoration of the person's physical, emotional, spiritual, and mental health and wellbeing. It's a deep restorative method that heals the inner spirit, allowing it to empower the other aspects of a person's being. Often physical and mental illnesses are caused by the ailments of the soul. The longer this goes unnoticed, the more the spirit will try to get the person's attention by manifesting in the form of illnesses or injuries. Given that the main component in Reiki healing is energy, who better to receive the power from than a powerful being like Archangel Michael. The following Reiki session will help you connect with Archangel Michael to receive his guidance and protection on your self-healing journey.

Instructions:

1. The first step here is asking for Reiki energy. Remember, Michael won't just start showering you with energy. He needs your permission to do that, so make sure to set an intention and make a conscious effort to welcome his light.

2. Prepare the tools you'll be using. This step is optional, as you won't necessarily have to use any if you don't want to. However, beginners might benefit from energy-channeling tools like crystals and symbols. Use the ones associated with Archangel Michael, such as blue crystals, images of swords, feathers, etc.

3. Prepare your body and mind to work with the Archangel's light. He will help you open channels of divine wisdom and help you communicate with the spiritual world during healing sessions. However, for the most profound healing, you must be prepared for his presence.

4. Assume a comfortable position and close your eyes. Focus on channeling your intention of inviting Michael's energy. Think about him sitting in front of you, with his hand extended,

channeling healing energy towards you.

5. He might send you a personal message to guide you in your self-healing journey. If you do not receive a message, don't worry. Just focus on the sensations his energy is evoking in your body.
6. Feel the deep peace and calm in your body and mind. You feel so light, almost as if you could lift off the surface you're currently on. You're filled with love, comfort, and renewed energy.
7. If you wish, recite a prayer to Michael to thank him for his blessings. You can also use this prayer as a reminder of your strength and courage that stems from the knowledge that Michael is always there to guide you.
8. Here is a prayer you can recite to the Archangel Michael:

"I call you to me, Michael,

And I welcome your divine presence.

Please help me discard the worries from my life.

Shine your light and warmth onto me

In any shadows that lurk within my energies.

So that I can heal and have a fertile and productive life

And everything I create is infused with love, happiness, and freedom of all ailments."

9. As you become receptive to Michael's energies, consider all the good it represents. It will boost your confidence in healing yourself and chase away all the emotional burdens hindering your recovery.
10. Remember, love is stronger than any other force. Michael loves you and will always stay close to you if you need him to be. He will help you banish whatever is affecting your energies and reclaim your health and happiness.

Feel free to do whatever you want when receiving Reiki energy empowered by the Archangel Michael. You can sit, lie, and even engage in activities like reading or meditation. The only requirement is to have an open mind and be prepared to receive the healing energy. At one point, you will feel it flowing toward you; make sure not to resist. Healing energy is as powerful as Archangel Michael's and can be overwhelming. Still, do your best to embrace it. sooner you do, the sooner it can play its role in transforming your health and wellbeing. During or after receiving the energy, you might feel a warm, tingling sensation coursing through your body, a buzzing in your head. It might also happen that you don't feel anything at all. This is entirely normal, too, especially for beginners who aren't receptive yet to the full scope of the energy. Some people also report feeling tired after receiving Reiki. This is a sign that Michael's light has taken its effects and is now empowering you to heal yourself. Healing activates an additional metabolic process, which requires more physical energy, and that can make you tired. Reiki energy can also trigger some unwanted feelings or memories. If this happens to you, just acknowledge them, and let the healing energy sweep them out.

Archangel Michael Healing Meditation for Your Body

Due to his powerful energy and status, Archangel Michael has a highly evolved spiritual essence, capable of restoring spiritual and physical bonds. He will do the same for you if you treat him with respect, honesty, and understanding. It will empower you to heal your physical body from illnesses and injuries.

Instructions:
1. Focus your attention by thinking about what you need assistance with. Are you dealing with a chronic condition or an acute one? Does it affect a specific part of your body or the entire body? The more specific you are when making a request for physical healing, the better.
2. The more Michael knows about your condition, the better. He will be able to channel his energy where you need it the most, and neither of you will waste any time during your healing journey.
3. Michael only works for the highest good. If he feels that you need to learn a certain lesson before healing you (or whomever you want to heal), he won't help you until you've learned it. If you're sure the timing is right, you can proceed.

4. Close your eyes and call upon Archangel Michael. Channel his light and trust in its power to improve your life.
5. Imagine an orb of light blue light in front of your mind's eye. Chant Michael's name three times while gazing into the light to open your energy field.
6. Bring your awareness to the issue you need assistance with and allow the blue light to surround you. As you're enveloped in this blue bubble, you feel that it acts like a shield.
7. Ask Michael to eliminate all the negative energies causing the physical symptoms. You might see him cut unwanted energetic ties with his sword around the affected body part or around your entire body.
8. As he releases you from the unwanted bonds, you might feel your body tense, with your shoulder and back straightening, standing upright like you would be one of Michael's angelic soldiers. This is a sign that you're ready to fight off whatever is ailing your body.
9. Now thank Michael by repeating the following message:

    "Archangel Michael

    I summon you now to guide and shield me on my healing journey.

    To give me strength and confidence that I can find my highest power.

    Send me signs that you have heard my voice

    And that I am protected in your love.

    Thank you for all the blessings you bestowed upon me today."
10. Slowly let the image of Michael and his energy fade and return to the present. Whenever you feel weighed down by your physical symptoms, remember your connection with Michael; he will be there to lift you up and help you overcome your challenges.

Healing Light Meditation with Archangel Michael

By summoning the Archangel's light, you can heal your energy and keep it healthy regardless of your emotional and spiritual challenges. It's a simple yet deep exercise that will help you empower yourself spiritually and be in a better condition to defeat health challenges.

Instructions:

1. Find a secluded place where you won't be disturbed and get comfortable. Close your eyes and deepen your breath. Continue breathing deeply until you feel focused on the present moment.

2. Notice your connection to the surface beneath you. Relax your shoulders and raise your palms up toward the sky as if you're ready to receive whatever blessing you'll receive.

3. When you're ready, close your eyes. Focus on your intention of welcoming Archangel Michael into your space and asking him to heal your energy. Open your mind and heart to receive his energy.

4. Gently and smoothly breathe in through your nose and out through your mouth a few times. Allow your breath to return to its normal rhythms, relax your abdomen and let everything go until your mind is still.

5. Allow your body to feel the energy in and around it. This will help it prepare to receive Michael's healing energy. Then, repeat the following words:

   "Across time and space, call upon Archangel Michael To be here with me today.

   Michael, I ask you to come with unconditional love

   May you also bring your light, peace, and protection

   Please help me to remove dark, unhealthy energies

   Asst me in cutting out energetic influences that don't benefit my health

   Guide me toward my own unique light,

   And the unconditional love that resides within me.

   Thank you."

6. Take a deep breath and imagine a beautiful aura surrounding you. It has a blue light; feel its energy and allow it to wash over your body. You're held safely within the light.

7. The blue light indicates that Michael is near. Call him closer to you. State what you need from him and remain open to

receiving his guidance and blessings. Feel him empowering your aura with his protective light.

8. Michael tells you that you're safe. Use this reassurance to focus on healing instead of worrying about defending yourself from malicious energies. Feel the energy seeping into your body, above and all around you, as they are infused into your aura.

9. Absorb the healing energy and take a few deep breaths to solidify the newly found energized feeling in your body and mind. Think about the unhealthy feelings and energies you no longer want to hold onto.

10. Ask Michael to remove the unwanted energies. Imagine the angel holding a sword above your head, lowering it, and tracing the protective aura around your body. He cuts away the unwanted energetic ties, allowing your body and mind to become stronger.

11. Feel the difference it makes not to have those unwanted energies. As you take a deep breath, you feel lighter and freer. Breathe in Michael's energy. The deeper you connect to his protective energies, the longer its effects will be on your healing.

12. Ask him to bless you with the energy of confidence and wisdom to overcome your health challenges. You can say this out loud or in your mind; Michael will hear you either way.

13. See your blue aura get brighter and brighter as your confidence and wisdom increase. You feel that you'll be supported through your health journey. You'll have Michael as a compass in difficult times, and he will provide you with your strength.

14. Sit and observe the sensation passing through your body. Allow yourself to be confident that you're at the right place at the right time on your journey.

15. Take a few breaths, and if the powerful energy flow you've previously received made your body tense up, relax it. Feel the aura you built with Michael and think about it as a permanent connection to him and all the healing energies of the universe.

16. Thank him for the blessings you've received and for remaining by your side through your health journey. Remember to tap into your aura when you need angelic

support in healing, and you'll be immediately connec
Archangel Michael.

Archangel Michael Complete Health Reset Meditation

As the chief of the Archangels and the governor of the Sun, Archangel Michael can empower your healing journey. He can also help you do a complete reset to restore your health and vitality. It's like boosting your immunity, metabolism, mental processes, and spiritual health all at once.

Instructions:

1. Find a comfortable position and close your eyes. Move your focus inward, let go of mundane thoughts and concentrate on your intention.
2. Visualize an orb of light appearing in front of you. That is the light of Archangel Michael. The angel will soon appear in front of you.
3. Take a moment to sense your inner connection with the Archangel. You can do this by focusing on your breath. Think of your breath as your inner spirit. By encouraging it to flow freely, you're creating a connection to the spiritual energies around you.
4. With each breath you release, the spirit within you becomes more connected to the space around you. You're now connected to your inner spirit.
5. Find any unwanted areas in your spirit, and release them when exhaling. Let go of your worries and feel the protective energy of Michael.
6. Now, guide your inner vision towards your inner light, the light of spiritual connection and communication. See it in your body. As your body lights up, it becomes stronger and stronger.
7. Observe Archangel Michael and feel his essence. Pay attention to the sensation in your body or any other signs the Archangel might send you. You might see a light that appears in front of your mind's eye.

8. When you feel connected to Michael, invite his blue aura to come to you. Welcome it as it envelopes you, seeping into your spiritual, mental, and spiritual being. You feel cherished and protected.

9. In Michael's blue light, you're held safely, but you might become aware of any worry or other negative feelings still present. This is normal, don't judge these sensations; just allow them to be. Michael will see them and use his light to cleanse them.

10. Think of your breath as a connection to his light. Think of how every breath you take removes those negative sensations. Once they're gone, Michael's shield will be put in place, preventing them from returning again.

11. Allow your awareness to travel out of your body and into the space around you. Let it go higher and higher until it travels as far as it can go. Enjoy yourself floating in space.

12. The Archangel Michael removes energy blockages within your body, mind, and spirit. He will remind you that when you call upon him, he will come.

13. Allow yourself to fully feel Michael's protection, knowing that it will empower your overall health and wellbeing. Feel the release of this complete energetic renewal.

14. Visualize Michael's blue light shining onto you. He raises his arms and wings, the light of his power beaming onto you, channeling light, love, protection, and restoration.

15. Feel the light filling your entire being. See your chakras shine brighter. Any negative energy trapped in the chakras dissolves, facilitating healing processes in your energetic body.

16. Your body begins to feel free of tension and pain. New healing paths are opening up in your mind and soul. Feel empowered, free, and open to the truth and grace angelic blessings represent.

17. Embrace the gifts you've received. They might be intense, but they are very much needed. Michael placed a shield of protection onto you, your energy feeling surrounded and empowered by his protective and healing energies.

18. Take a moment to think about the messages you've received from Michael and slowly let go of your focus on your intention. Take a few deep breaths to return to your body and become aware of your physical sensations again.

Chapter 6: Banishing Negative Energy

Archangel Michael can be called upon to banish existing negative energies. This chapter is dedicated to practical methods you can use to expel negative energies from your body, mind, and spirit, your environment, your life, and the life of your loved ones. From asking for Michael's help during cleansing rituals to making banishing salt and sigils, there are plenty of ways this Archangel can help you eliminate unwanted influences from and around your energy field.

Cleansing Ritual to Banish Negative Energy

This cleansing ritual will help you banish negative energy from people, items, and your home or office space. It's a deep spiritual cleansing method recommended for first-time energetic sweeping and preparation for major rituals, ceremonies, and festivities. You can also use it when you feel overwhelmed by malicious energies and can't seem to move forward without banishing them.

Ingredients:
- 4 blue or red candles
- A lighter (avoid matches as they're made with sulfur, which is associated with evil spirits)
- Candle holder for each candle

- Incense (optional) – myrrh or frankincense work best for energetic purging

Instructions:

1. Find a place where you won't be disturbed. Turn off your phone. If you're doing this at home and have small children or pets, do this in a room away from them. If you stop the banishing process midway through, it won't work.

2. Focus on setting a strong state of mind so that you can keep going whatever happens. Keep in mind that depending on the strength of the negative energies you're dealing with, they might try to resist, and you have to be stronger than them.

3. Before you can meet Michael, set an intention of asking him to assist you so he knows what you are about to do and so that he can join you. If you wish, you can even pray to him or meditate with him the day before and share your intention and ask for his protection ahead of time.

4. Place the candles at the four corners of your space (depending on the area you want to cleanse). If you're purging your body, place them in the four corners of the space you'll be occupying during the ritual. If a corner has a closed space (like a closet), place a candle as close as possible. Keep the candles away from papers, drafts, curtains, and other safety hazards. The candles might spark due to the influences of the energies you're about to banish.

5. If you're cleansing your home, you'll light the candle nearest to the front door or the door you use most often first. Start with the candle closest to the door if you're cleaning a room. If you're cleansing yourself or an item, start with the one closest to your left or the left of the item you want to purify.

6. If you're using incense, light it before the candles. If not, move on to lighting the candles one by one. When you light the first one, recite the following prayer:

"Archangel Michael, defend me in this battle

When I am trying to protect myself against the wickedness,

And eliminate evil influences from (whatever you're cleansing).

I pray to you, Oh prince of the angels, by the power of the creator,

Help me banish the evil spirits who seek the ruin of my life and work."

7. Repeat the prayer two more times and call upon Michael, asking for his assistance in banishing the malevolent energies.

8. Moving in a counterclockwise direction, light the second candle. While you do, repeat the prayer from above three times. Generally, you would face toward the outer perimeter of the space because you want to expel negativity. However, if you want to banish negativity that causes disharmony among people in the space, face inward.

9. After each candle you light, repeat the prayer three times and make your request to Archangel Michael. Open a door or window when you reach the last candle and complete the last request.

10. If you're cleansing yourself or another person, you or they should stand as close to the door or window as possible. If you're cleansing an item, move it closer to the opened exit.

11. Making a sweeping gesture outward helps with dispelling the negative energy as quickly as possible. As you do, imagine all these influences as black or gray smoke, leaving the space/person/item you wish to cleanse. Then, say the following:

"In the name of Archangel Michael,

I sweep out all negative energy

and discord from my presence."

12. Repeat the line above nine times while continuing with the sweeping motion. Then, turn around, face inward, and say the following nine times:

"In the name of Archangel Michael,

May the banished energies be replaced,

With the power of angels

And other protective and benevolent spirits.

May Michael guide me in the future,

As I attempt to ward off negative and evil influences.

May this (space/person/item) be filled with divine light."

13. Allow the candles to burn down completely, but don't leave them unattended. Extinguish them whenever you can't stay near them.

Depending on the size of the candles you're using, they can take up to a week to burn down (even more if you're extinguishing them several times a day). Extinguish them only by snuffing them out. Never blow them, as this is insulting to the heavenly fire.

14. When relighting the candles, move again in a counterclockwise direction, saying the prayer from above once for each candle. This will recharge them with your original intentions.

15. After a successful cleansing, you'll notice that the atmosphere around the item, person, or space is lighter. They might have a light aura around them and are easier to use/get along with. You have a sense of peace and wellbeing whenever you're near the person/item/space you've purified.

16. If you don't notice any changes, you might still have some negative energies left over. In this case, you must repeat the ritual. Suppose your work involves regular encounters with evil influences. In that case, it's a good idea to regularly clean your tools, yourself, and your space.

If you can't light a candle in the space you want to purify, you can perform the ritual elsewhere. Writing the name of the unclean space on a piece of paper and under the candles is an excellent alternative to banish unwanted energies. Michael will still know where you want to enact the banishment and will help you do it effectively.

Evocation to Banish Evil

Archangel Michael is the best ally in warding off evil spiritual forces and dispelling them from yourself and your environment. Evil forces always threaten to overcome your soul, but Michael can help you fight them. By building a stronger connection with the Archangel, you'll always be able to keep those negative influences working tirelessly against you in check. This involves regular evocations for banishment. The following prayer is one of the best tools for this purpose.

Instructions:

1. In a secluded area, find a comfortable position and focus on your intention of invoking Archangel Michael to assist you.

2. Take a deep breath, and close your eyes to fully direct your attention to your task. Either aloud or in your mind, call out to Michael. Chant his name several times.

3. When you can see him in front of your mind's eyes, address him with this prayer:

"I welcome you, Archangel Michael, the heavenly host who stands in front of me.

Ready to assist me in my quest to fight the evil forces.

You who valiantly defend me against harm and destruction,

I earnestly entreat you to assist me also

in this painful and perilous conflict I have found myself in against my spiritual foe.

I ask you to join me, Archangel Michael, and allow me to fight courageously

And banish evil spirits, whom you have already overthrown,

and whom I can also completely overcome

Help me triumph over the enemy of my salvation,

May you be with me in all the battles I have yet to fight. "

Creating Banishing Salt

Banishing salt is a great way to spiritually cleanse your living or work environments. It is easy to make from ingredients you might already have in your kitchen pantry or get from a grocery store, and it can absorb any energy you channel into it. For example, you can ask Archangel Michael to enhance your salt recipe, making whatever work you use it for more effective. Most banishing salt recipes require a mixture of herbs (dry or fresh), essential oils, and some form of natural salt. The following recipe uses rosemary, lavender, and sea salt, all of which are known for their spiritually purifying effects.

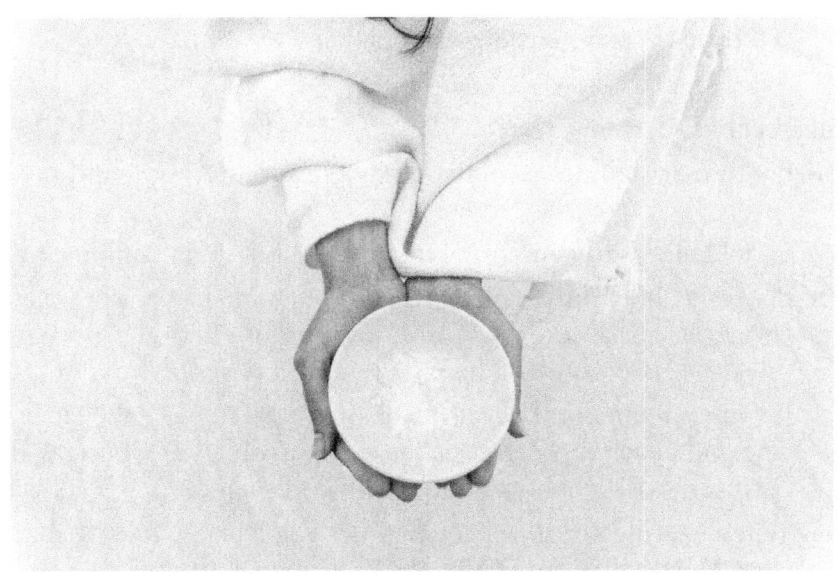

Banishing salt is used to cleanse your work or home.
https://unsplash.com/photos/Tlcy2YCFwlg

As one of the world's oldest herbal cleansers, rosemary has been used to banish evil influences for several thousand years. Many cultures used it in combination with spiritual evocations, making it suitable for asking for Michael's assistance too. You can use it to cleanse your mind, body, and spirit, do consecration rituals, and release negative energies. Lavender can be used for similar purposes and to bring you peace, tranquility, happiness, and joy. These emotions empower your energies, allowing them to cleanse your entire being more effectively. Michael's protective powers can give you peace, but they can also amplify the soothing properties of lavender. He can also help you channel the herb's soothing properties for better focus during spiritual work. You can remain vigilant to protect yourself from negative influences and banish any that enter your space as soon as possible. Sea salt has a rejuvenating effect on your mind, body, and spirit. It can also purify your home and items you use for spiritual work. You can use banishing salts to remove unwanted energies from your home, an object, your body, or another person's body (in baths).

Ingredients:
- 1 fresh rosemary sprig (or a tablespoon of dried herb)
- 1 fresh lavender sprig (or a tablespoon of dried herb)
- 1 cup of rock sea salt

- 4 drops of frankincense essential oil
- 1 decorative bowl

Instructions:

1. Put the salt and the essential oil in a decorative bowl, and mix the two.
2. Sprinkle the herbs on top of the mixture but don't combine them.
3. Place the bowl in the area where you want to banish negativity from. Keep it in a safe place, away from children and pets. A great place to put it is a high shelf in the corner of the room.
4. If you want to banish negativity from an object, place the latter into the salt bowl and let it sit there for a while. It's best to do it overnight or eight hours before using the item.
5. When placing the bowl into its designed place, ask Michael to assist you with your intention. Call upon him and address him with the following prayer:

   "Archangel Michael, I ask that you enrich this salt with love and light,

   So, I can use it to trap all the negative energy in this space/item/person

   And banish it forever. Thank you!"

6. Allow the salt to attract the negative energies for some time. It acts as a magnet for evil, so depending on how much negativity is lurking around, this might take a few days.
7. If necessary, you can repeat the process by preparing a new mixture to trap even more negativity. Alternatively, you can place several small bowls around; this works faster in larger spaces.
8. If you're using salt to banish negativity from your body or another person's body, sprinkle it into the bath water and soak it for at least 30 minutes.
9. When the salt has had time to act, take it and toss it out of your home, along with the negativity. Make sure it leaves your environment to effectively banish unwanted energies.

Creating a Banishing Sigil

The sigil of Archangel Michael is a powerful symbol to use in banishing ceremonies and rituals. As with any sign associated with this angel, the sigil can be used to invoke him, communicate with him directly, and ask for any assistance you need. While plenty of Archangel Michael sigils are available for the best effects, creating one of your own is recommended. It takes some practice but isn't terribly hard to do. And once you master how to make it, you'll have a powerful tool for any ritual or spiritual exercises you might want to include Michael in. For example, you can use it when requesting protection from the Archangel. The sigil infused with Michael's power can be carved into objects and become a talisman for personal protection against evil forces. It can be etched into candles to empower any prayer, meditation, or invocation you use it for. You can draw it on a piece of paper and incorporate it into your work or make a large-scale copy of it and use it as a foundation for a crystal grid empowered by Archangel Michael.

Instructions:
1. Find and prepare (print out) a Rose Wheel symbol, preferably one without any modern additions. You can also draw one by copying one that suits your purposes. You'll also need the letters from the Hebrew version of Michael's name.

The rose wheel symbol.
https://www.needpix.com/photo/892366/symbol-wind-rose-nautica-free-vector-graphics

2. Mark the letters of Michael's name on the Rose Wheel and connect the points going from the first letter to the last (right to left). While you do this, focus on your intention, in this case, banishing negativity.
3. You've now created an Archangel Michael sigil infused with your intention. The next step is to prepare yourself and your space before using the sigil.
4. Take a cleansing bath and purify your space with incense or smudging. Now charge your sign with your energy by holding it close to your body and focusing on your intuition. This will activate it.
5. Next, you can pray, meditate, or simply prepare your sacred space by lighting a candle, placing crystals, or doing anything else you wish before summoning Michael.
6. Call Archangel Michael and ask him to help banish negativity from your life. If you have any questions on how to do it, ask them now. Listen to any messages you receive from the angel.
7. Follow the angel's advice. He will help you banish evil forces.

Deep Spiritual Cleansing with Archangel Michael

This spiritual cleansing and awakening ritual incorporates prayer for calling upon Archangel Michael and the enlightened beings working with him to free you from all negative energetic influences, clearing your aura and chakras from limitations and blockages caused by malicious energies. It can act against both known and unknown influences. For the best effects, repeat it for 21 consecutive days. Each day, you'll ask Archangel Michael to join you as you cleanse yourself from all negativities, and this will strengthen your bond with him.

Instructions:
1. Find a comfortable position in a place where you won't be disturbed for a few minutes. Close your eyes and take deep breaths until you can eliminate all unwanted thoughts from your mind and focus solely on your intuition.
2. Call on Archangel Michael by chanting his name three times aloud. When he arrives, recite the following prayer:

"I appeal to you, Michael, to calm my fears,

And eliminate the forces that interfere with my goals and life's purpose.

I reach into my higher self and close my aura,

Leaving my energies open to only you, Michael,

I appeal to you to seal and protect my energies,

Banishing all negativity from them."

3. Imagine your auric field surrounded by Michael's protective shield. Feel how it repels any energies coming from the outside. Reach into your higher self, and see yourself connecting with Michael's shield.

4. Once your higher self can tap into Michael's shield, bring your awareness to any unwanted energies lurking in your soul. Use your connection to the shield to banish these. See them leaving your body as a dark cloud, pushed out from the bright light surrounding you.

5. Next, ask Michael to remove all the other unwanted spiritual influences he can detect. Remember, there are often far more negative energies hindering your spiritual growth than you are aware of at any given moment. Fortunately, Michael can remove even these energies.

6. Ask Michael to remove self-imposed limitations too. Then, request that he restores your energetic balance. Imagine him going over your chakras, restoring their functions, balancing your aura, and reinstating your natural psychic defenses.

7. Ask him to remove past influences, present disturbances, and possible future ones too. While he can't protect you from all the negativity you'll encounter in the future, he can banish the ones that have roots in the present.

8. He will infuse you with divine energy and free you from all those ties and associations that no longer serve you. By empowering you with the highest energy, he ensures that your energies will be working for the higher good and the good of your health and wellbeing.

9. Take a few moments to observe the sensations you feel in your body. You might feel warm, light, and happy. You might be elated and tired at the same time. However, you know that

you're now free of the remnants of all unwanted energies, and your energy vibrates higher.

10. Through these higher vibrations, you can feel Michael's energy clearer than ever. Thank Michael, and dedicate your future work to honor him for this majestic blessing he has given you. Tell him that he is free to warn and assist you whenever you need spiritual cleansing in the future.

11. Slowly let the image of Michael fade, and your mind be filled with mundane thoughts as you return to the present moment. Take a few moments to feel your renewed energy and spiritual attunement and think about all the good you can do now that you're free of unwanted ties and evil influences.

Chapter 7: Crystals to Connect with Archangel Michael

In this chapter, you will understand what crystals are and how they work. You'll find out how they correspond with the chakra system and how you can use them to improve your overall wellbeing. This chapter also explains how you can use crystals to connect with Archangel Michael and ask for his support and guidance. Finally, you'll know which crystals to use when working with this higher power.

Crystals correspond with the chakra system, and you can use them to connect with Archangel Michael.
https://www.pexels.com/photo/white-and-gray-stone-on-brown-wooden-table-3610752/

What Are Crystals and How Do They Work?

If you're into alternative or holistic healing methods, you've likely heard of crystal healing before. Practitioners believe that when selected and used correctly, crystals can channel the healing energy of the surrounding environment. They can generate positive and revitalizing vibrations and improve your overall mental, emotional, physical, and spiritual state.

Each crystal uniquely impacts the mind, soul, and body, depending on its color and makeup. Each stone emits different vibrations based on its structure and the way that its atoms vibrate and interact with each other. Your body is an electromagnetic structure: energy not only flows throughout it, but it's also radiated and influenced by your thoughts, feelings, and spiritual wellbeing. As long as you don't suffer from an ailment that requires medical intervention, crystals offer an interesting and fun way to channel that energy toward better health.

Approximately 99.9% of all matter is empty space occupied by energy. It is everywhere around us. Inanimate objects like tables, books, phones, and of course, crystals are made of vibrating energy. Everything in the world, including humans and any other living being, has a unique vibrational frequency.

Think of vibrational frequency as a spectrum. People on the lower end are full of negative, unwanted emotions like anxiety and anger. They're often controlled by fear and can't see the positive aspects of life. People on the higher end, on the other hand, emit positivity, love, and compassion. They enjoy peace of mind and always see the cup half full.

Vibrational energies, however, are very volatile. If you have a high vibrational frequency today, this doesn't necessarily mean that you will in a month. Your vibrations fluctuate several times a day because your interactions with others influence them, the content you consume, the events that happen throughout the day, your memories, the news you receive, and so on.

Crystals, unlike humans, have a stable vibrational frequency. Their perfect, fixed, and repetitive geometric structures allow them to maintain their energy. The more stable a vibrational frequency is, the more powerful it is. Since vibrational frequencies can influence the energies around them, you can benefit from using a crystal's stable energy to influence your own.

Even though scientific studies don't back the effectiveness of crystal healing in curing physical ailments, crystals have been used to enhance people's wellbeing for millennia. There are accounts of ancient Egyptians, Greeks, Romans, Indians, and Chinese using crystals to protect themselves in potentially dangerous situations and to treat certain medical ailments. If it worked for past civilizations, then it's not crazy to think that it can help humans today.

Crystals can also help people through the power of color therapy. While there is no scientific evidence that color therapy can cure physical ailments, it can support mental health treatment. Each shade of color radiates rays that have a certain effect on people's bodily responses and, therefore, their behavior. This effect occurs because the sun, the main source of energy on Earth, emits all the colors of the rainbow. While this blend of colors results in white light, it's the only reason so many colors can be seen in the world. Like the sun, Gems have and emit energy and color, which is why they respond to light.

If you use a prism to look at the sun's rays, you'll see infrared and ultraviolet, which are invisible to the naked eye, along with the seven colors of the rainbow. These nine colors are the core energies of the solar system, and the eight planets and Pluto all resonate with them.

Each planet radiates a wavelength of colored light that matches the wavelength of the light emitted from its corresponding crystal. When placed near the body, the crystal absorbs these solar wavelengths and energies and radiates them into the body. This encourages the targeted chakra to become balanced, improving the individual's overall health.

Each color has unique qualities and affects a different aspect of your life. Purple, for instance, has a higher frequency than red. If you look up an image of the chakra system, you'll find that the crown chakra, which is the one with the highest vibrational frequency, is purple. Conversely, the root chakra, which has the lowest vibration, is red.

Each chakra and its corresponding color share vibrational frequencies, so you need to determine the physical, mental, or emotional symptoms you wish to fix or the areas in your life that you want to elevate. This will allow you to determine the responsible chakra and choose a crystal in the color that matches it. For example, if you struggle with self-expression, you might need to restore balance to your throat chakra. In that case, you'll work with sapphires. If you feel unstable in life or are struggling to overcome certain challenges, you should opt for red carnelian, for instance, to activate your root chakra.

There are 114 chakras, or energy centers, in the body. The most important and popular ones are these seven: the Root (Muladhara) Chakra, Sacral (Svadhisthana) Chakra, Solar Plexus (Manipura) Chakra, Heart (Anahata) Chakra, Throat (Visuddha) Chakra, Third Eye (Ajna) Chakra, and Crown (Sahasrara) Chakra. Each one is associated with different organs and spiritual, emotional, mental, and bodily functions.

Since the root chakra has the lowest vibrational frequency, it's associated with the basic elements of life. It is concerned with a person's sense of security and safety. Each chakra represents a deeper aspect of living than the previous one. Blockages or imbalances in the chakras can manifest as emotional dysregulation, mental issues, or physical ailments.

The Crystals to Use for Each Chakra

- **The Root Chakra:** It corresponds with the color red and represents the quality of being grounded and "rooted" in the Earth. It's also associated with a person's sense of safety, security, and survival.

    You can work with crystals like tourmaline, malachite, red carnelian, Smokey quartz, ruby, red tiger's eye, red calcite, hematite, red jasper, red quartz, and garnet.

- **The Sacral Chakra:** It's shown in orange and represents a person's energy or inclination to pursue pleasure, creativity, activity, procreation, and desire.

    It's associated with crystals like orange calcite, amber, tangerine quartz, goldstone, sunstone, bronzite, peach moonstone, orange selenite, and brecciated Jasper.

- **The Solar Plexus Chakra:** Its color is yellow, and it is associated with your confidence, inner wisdom, and assertiveness.

    Opt for crystals like citrine, tiger's eye, yellow jasper, heliodor, bumblebee jasper, rutilated quartz, pyrite, and yellow Aventurine.

- **The Heart Chakra:** Its color is green, and it is responsible for the love you express towards yourself and others.

    To work with the Heart Chakra, you need crystals like malachite, green opal, green aventurine, rhodonite, rose quartz, pink tourmaline, prehnite, and amazonite.

- **The Throat Chakra:** It is blue and associated with a person's ability to kindly and clearly express their truth.

  Blue calcite, blue kyanite, blue lace agate, celestite, angelite, sodalite, aquamarine, turquoise, and aqua aura quartz are examples of crystals you can use.

- **The Third Eye Chakra:** Its color is indigo, and it's associated with intuition, memory, and imagination.

  Amethyst, lapis lazuli, lepidolite, iolite, labradorite, fluorite, and apatite are among the crystals you can use.

- **The Crown Chakra:** It is violet and associated with your consciousness and spiritual connection and transformation.

You can work with crystals like moonstone, geode, amethyst, ametrine, clear quartz, howlite, lepidolite, scolecite, charoite, rainbow fluorite, Herkimer diamond, and danburite.

How These Crystals Can Help You Connect with Higher Powers

Thanks to their energetic properties, crystals can help people connect with spiritual realms and higher powers. Their makeup allows them to influence and interact with subdued energies. When you use the right crystals for each aspect of your life and work on balancing all your chakras, you can increase your vibrational frequency.

According to the law of attraction, you attract people and situations that align with your vibrational frequency. To interact with anyone around you, you must both have the same or at least similar frequencies. To connect with the spiritual realm, you must achieve a lighter, clearer, and higher vibrational frequency. This requires you to make several changes to your life, such as eliminating sources of negativity, maintaining a positive outlook, improving your sleep and diet, staying active, nourishing your mind and soul, and engaging in self-care.

While they might not be enough, especially if you're starting at a very low vibrational frequency, crystals can be a good place to start because they're energy amplifiers. As long as you have clear intentions, crystals can make connecting with the spiritual realm easier. However, for this to work, you need to keep your thoughts and feelings aligned with your intentions. If you wish to connect with Archangel Michael, you must clarify this intention at the beginning of your spiritual practice. Make it the focus of your session, know in your heart that it's possible, and keep your thoughts positive. If you feel or think that you won't succeed, this will likely block your manifestation.

Crystals also serve as symbolic representations of higher powers and spiritual entities. They have been incorporated into rituals and presented as offerings since the beginning of time. Each spiritual entity is associated with a crystal that represents the qualities and radiates the energy that they possess. Working with crystals that correspond with Archangel Michael can help you tune into his vibrational frequency and invoke some of his qualities. Crystals are also considered physical representations of the connection you have with higher powers. They help bridge the worldly and spiritual realms, reminding you that this interaction is possible.

How to Connect with Archangel Michael Using Crystals

There isn't a set of rules that you should follow when connecting with archangels or other spiritual entities. Spiritual connections are very personal and intuitive processes. While some tools and practices (such as using crystals) can facilitate the connection, you need to know that the interaction itself is built on your intentions, faith, intuition, beliefs, and alignment.

When working with Archangel Michael, it helps to choose crystals that resonate with his energy and align with your needs. If you can't find a crystal that serves both purposes, you should trust your intuition. Your mind, body, and consciousness know what they need and will lead you to the right choice. If you're unsure what to do, you can work with a crystal that traditionally represents Archangel Michael to invoke his energy and strengths and call on him for guidance.

You should also create a sacred space for your spiritual practices. Dedicate a comfortable and quiet spot in your home for all your connections with Archangel Michael. You can set up an altar or simply decorate a space with images of swords, feathers, scales, or other objects that represent him. Keep your chosen crystal on the altar or near you to facilitate your connection.

Set a clear intention to connect with Archangel Michael. You can practice breathing or other grounding or mindfulness exercises to maintain your focus if you're struggling with intrusive thoughts and feelings. Make sure that your intentions are true and genuine. You can verbally or mindfully state that you wish to connect with Archangel Michael to receive his support, guidance, or protection.

Get in a comfortable position and take a few deep breaths. Close your eyes and only start when you feel centered. Hold your chosen crystal or crystals close to your body. You can bring them close to your heart or third eye chakra to heighten your intuition.

Imagine a sphere of divine light growing around you and blessing you with positive feelings, compassion, and protection. Call on Archangel Michael out loud or in your head, inviting him into your space. Repeat your intention and state the reason you're invoking his presence.

Don't hesitate to repeat your words if you feel you should. Lean into your intuitions and be mentally and emotionally open to receiving any messages, new thoughts, revelations, or sensations during your meditation or prayer. You will likely feel a shift in your surrounding energy once he responds to your efforts. His guidance will likely manifest through your inner wisdom or knowledge.

Express your gratitude towards Archangel Michael once you're done with your spiritual practice. This will show him that you appreciate his guidance and strengthen your connection. Make sure to cleanse your crystal before and after all your spiritual practices using water, salt, sunlight, moonlight, or smudging techniques.

Crystals You Can Use

- **Clear Quartz:** Clear quartz is a multi-purpose, powerful crystal that you can use to charge and cleanse your other stones because it absorbs energy from the sun. Clear quartz is known for its healing properties, as it replenishes one's body and soul. This stone amplifies the energies of other crystals and intensifies people's thoughts and intentions, which enhances manifestation. It also makes it easier to connect with supernatural entities and get in touch with the spiritual realm since it can channel their energy. Carrying around this crystal will help you align with your thoughts and body. It can also bring peace and positive energy to your home if you keep it there.

- **Lapis Lazuli**: This deep blue crystal is speckled with flakes of gold. It's associated with Archangel Michael because of its color and can greatly support your spiritual practice. Working with lapis lazuli can activate your third eye chakra, allowing you to connect with your intuition and higher wisdom. This can make it easier to connect with Archangel Michael and other spiritual entities. Lapis lazuli enhances truthful communication within oneself and in social interactions. Working with this stone boosts an individual's self-awareness and encourages them to be honest and frank.
- **Sugilite**: This stone is very rare, expensive, and difficult to acquire. This mesmerizing stone comes in rich shades of purple. Not only is it beautiful to look at, but it also offers tremendous spiritual support. This makes it one of the most sought-after gemstones in the world. Sugilite helps people reach out to angels and spirit guides and protects against negative situations, thoughts, and feelings. This crystal releases energy blockages in the body, making it easier to attain a balanced chakra system. Working with this crystal gives you the emotional and mental clarity you need to overcome difficulties with ease. It dissipates stress and anxiety and helps you develop peace of mind. Sugilite can help you reap the benefits of your meditation practices, facilitate healing, and bring attention to helpful insights. As it can boost one's awareness of the spiritual realm, sugilite is a very valuable tool for those who wish to engage in astral travel.
- **Amber:** Even though it's a fossilized tree resin and not exactly a crystal, amber is effective in enhancing psychic powers and alleviating anxiety. It also attracts abundance and good fortune. Amber is considered a healing crystal because it encourages the body to regenerate and fosters passion and strength. Its protective and solar energies create a suitable environment for connecting with Archangel Michael, who is also associated with protection and guidance.
- **Golden Topaz:** Like amber, golden topaz is connected to the sun. Working with this shiny yellow crystal will boost your vitality and raise your vibration, creating the ideal environment for connecting with the archangel. This stone is also associated with confidence, manifestation, and self-empowerment, which

allows you to invoke some of the strengths and energies of Archangel Michael. Meditating with this stone can also benefit your physical health as it helps relieve fatigue, indigestion, and the symptoms of arthritis. You can use this stone to manifest prosperity, good fortune, and abundance and support your astral travel efforts.

- **Sapphire:** This vivid blue crystal is associated with Archangel Michael and can open a communication channel with him. Working with this stone allows you to strengthen your intuition and access higher levels of knowledge and wisdom. Sapphire enhances mental clarity and activates the third eye chakra, which allows people to tap into their psychic abilities and become more receptive to otherworldly messages and communications. You can invoke the protective energy of Archangel Michael by working with sapphire to receive his guidance and protect yourself from negative influences. This crystal also helps with verbal and energetic communication and expression, leading to fruitful connections with the angelic realm.

- **Sodalite:** This beautiful blue crystal is characterized by its white streaks. It encourages you to lean into the guidance of your inner compass and even boosts your intuition and psychic abilities. Working with sodalite makes you more spiritually insightful, which deepens your connection with Archangel Michael. This stone can make you a better communicator, improve your focus, and enhance your mental clarity. People who struggle with anxiety and overthinking can benefit from incorporating this crystal into their meditative and spiritual practices. Like sapphire, you can use sodalite to call on Archangel Michael's protective and guiding energy.

- **Apatite:** Apatite comes in several colors, such as blue, yellow, and green. It's known to be the crystal of motivation, inspiration, and manifestation. You can work with this stone to clear your throat chakra and improve your communication and self-expression skills. Apatite is also associated with the third eye chakra, which enhances intuition and psychic abilities. Apatite can help you get in touch with your inner strength and courage, which are some of the qualities that Archangel Michael embodies.

- **Kyanite:** This indigo stone is popular thanks to its high vibration. It also has energy-clearing qualities and corresponds with truth and balance. Kyanite is associated with spiritual connection and transformation, which means that it can help you enhance your communication with higher powers and the spiritual world.

Your intuition is the key to connecting with Archangel Michael or any other higher power. Your intentions need to be sincere and genuine. You should also truly believe in your ability to invoke the Archangel and receive his guidance. While true power comes from within, crystals can support and facilitate your connection by amplifying your intention and refining your vibrational frequency.

Chapter 8: Herbs and Essential Oils of Archangel Michael

This chapter explores what essential oils are and how they work. You'll learn how to use herbs and essential oils to improve your overall wellbeing and balance your chakra system. You'll find out which oils correspond to each chakra and the various techniques you can use to activate your energy centers.

By reading this chapter, you'll understand why essential oils are powerful additions to your spiritual practices. You'll know how to use them to align your vibrational frequencies with those of the spiritual realm. You'll also learn how to use essential oils to work with Archangel Michael and other spiritual entities. Finally, you'll come across a list of essential oils that you can use to connect with the Archangel and learn about their qualities, benefits, and properties.

What Are Essential Oils and How Do They Work?

Essential oils are extracted from leaves, roots, flowers, herbs, and other parts of plants. Pure essential oils capture the entire essence of the plant, resulting in a potent elixir. The compounds in essential oils have strong, energetic vibrations, which is what makes them capable of curing the mind, body, and soul. Depending on the plant from which it was derived, each essential oil has unique healing properties, aromas, purposes, and vibrations.

Essential oils can be used to connect with spirits.
https://www.pexels.com/photo/two-clear-glass-bottles-with-liquids-672051/

Herbs and essential plants have been used to treat physical ailments for thousands of years. Many people still reach for anise to relieve their cough or chamomile if they're having trouble falling asleep. However, most people don't know that you can use herbs and essential oils to connect with spiritual entities and receive their guidance.

Each essential oil is characterized by certain strengths, qualities, and biological compounds that are associated with certain angelic energies. Just like Sapphire, for example, allows you to invoke some of Archangel Michael's strengths, the energetic frequency in Frankincense allows you to call on him for support. Over millennia of experimenting and examining the qualities of each essential oil, people started associating certain essential oils with specific Archangels.

Essential oils play an extensive role in spiritual practices. From serving as purifying and cleansing oils for your space and body to bridging between the physical and spiritual realms, essential oils are indispensable tools for spiritual growth and development. You can reap the full benefits of your meditations by incorporating aromatherapy into your practice or manifest your desires by setting clear intentions while using them as ointments.

Like crystals, essential oils have constant and stable vibrations. Most of them are characterized by their high vibrational frequencies and their light essence. Using them regularly allows you to influence your vibrations, gradually aligning them with the resonance of the vibrational realm.

Essential Oils and the Chakra System

While you can drink herbs or use tinctures to target certain ailments, you can enhance your overall wellbeing by using essential oils to balance your entire chakra system. Each chakra corresponds with a specific set of essential oils. You can create a schedule that allows you to work on each chakra on its own, starting from the root chakra and working your way up to the crown chakra. You can also determine your needs and areas in life you need to elevate, identify the chakras you need to balance, and work with the corresponding essential oils.

- **The Root Chakra:** Black pepper, vetiver, frankincense, patchouli, cedarwood, spikenard, and sandalwood
- **The Sacral Chakra:** Ylang-ylang, clary sage, orange, jasmine, rosewood, bergamot, neroli, and fennel
- **The Solar Plexus Chakra:** Lemongrass, ginger, clove, cinnamon, coriander, juniper, rosemary, grapefruit, mandarin, and roman chamomile
- **The Heart Chakra:** Rose, melissa, everlasting, eucalyptus, jasmine, yarrow, lemon, and marjoram
- **The Throat Chakra:** Geranium, jasmine, tea tree, peppermint, sage, frankincense, cypress, and clove
- **The Third Eye Chakra:** Palo santo, clary sage, rose, chamomile, bay laurel, carrot seed, jasmine, and geranium
- **The Crown Chakra:** Lotus, helichrysum, sandalwood, spikenard, cedarwood, benzoin, frankincense, and vetiver

Aromatherapy is one of the most effective ways of using essential oils. You can either inhale the aroma from the bottle or add a few drops to a diffuser. Diffusers are great because they purify your space and allow you to inhale the aroma for longer periods. The tiny molecules that you inhale will influence your energy flow and enhance your thoughts and feelings.

You can also use jojoba, coconut, or any other carrier oil to dilute your essential oil before applying it to the targeted chakra center. Massage your skin in a clockwise direction, close your eyes, and imagine that the chakra is activating and falling into balance. Make sure to test your skin for allergies or sensitivity before using each essential oil.

You can also add a few drops of the selected essential oil to your bath or on your washcloth as you shower. Bring your attention toward the chakra that you're targeting as you relax. Think about the qualities and the aroma of the essential oil and how it's contributing to your general health.

Incorporate essential oils into your regular meditation, visualization, or other mindfulness practices. Choose a comfortable and quiet space to practice, and add a few drops of essential oil to your diffuser. Visualize the chakra in a perfectly balanced, luminous state. Make it the center of your attention throughout the mindfulness session.

You should set a clear intention regardless of the method you choose. Maintain your focus on the chakra with which you are working and avoid engaging with any intrusive thoughts. You can engage in breathwork or grounding techniques before you start your practice to clear your mind and be fully present.

Keep in mind that essential oils alone aren't sufficient to balance your chakras and improve your health. You need to consult with a healthcare professional if you struggle with any medical or mental health issues. Essential oils are most effective when implemented into a holistic treatment program. Prioritize self-care, eat a healthy and balanced diet, get enough quality sleep, exercise regularly, get rid of unhealthy habits, and partake in uplifting activities.

Using Essential Oils to Work with Archangel Michael

You can use essential oils to work with any Archangel you want. To make the most of your practice, you must start by exploring the unique qualities, attributes, and roles of the archangel with whom you wish to connect. Explore their energy and understand what it would feel like to be in their presence.

Archangel Michael is usually portrayed as a defender and a warrior, which means that he's strong, courageous, and powerful. People usually call on him for his protective and supportive energies. Archangel Michael is also the leader of the angels and can help people overcome their fears and challenges. Identifying what Archangel Michael can help you with and the aspects of your life in which he can offer assistance will allow you to establish a meaningful connection.

You should consider the chakras you wish to balance and the qualities of your targeted Archangel when choosing essential oils. In most cases, you'll find a few fulfill both purposes. In that case, you should lean into your intuition when making your final decision. You can alternate between various essential oils and different application methods, but you should focus on a specific intention.

Using essential oils that align with Archangel Michael's qualities and energy will strengthen your connection and facilitate the invocation process. You should generally opt for essential oils that are associated with protection, reassurance, higher consciousness, and purification.

If you wish to establish a relationship with a higher power, you want to make your space as conducive to their presence as possible. Choose a quiet, comfortable, distraction-free space to dedicate to your spiritual endeavors. Cleanse the space by burning or smudging purifying herbs like sage or palo santo. This will help you get rid of negative energies and protect yourself and your space before you enter the spiritual realm. You can set up an altar and decorate the space with objects, crystals, and symbols associated with Archangel Michael to anchor your intention.

You should always start any spiritual practice by setting a clear intention. Get in a comfortable position and practice mindfulness techniques to clear your thoughts. Focus on your desire, close your eyes, and center yourself. Once you're ready, call upon Archangel Michael, either verbally or mentally. Explain that you wish to connect with him and that you're seeking his support, guidance, and protection. Keep your mind and heart open to any signs. Trust that they've successfully received and responded to your request. Trust your intuition and feel the slightest shift in the surrounding energy.

Essential oils can serve as physical and symbolic anchors for your intention. They can help you foster a deeper connection with the archangel. Use a carrier oil to dilute the essential oil before applying it to specific points of your body, such as the heart chakra, your temples, or your inner wrists. You can also rub it in a clockwise direction onto the chakra that you wish to work with. Imagine that a bridge has been formed, connecting you with Archangel Michael. Think about the qualities that you wish to invoke while inhaling the aroma.

Perform a meditation practice that puts your mind and body at ease. This will help you release the mental, physical, and emotional blocks that hinder this connection. Drop your shoulders, relax your jaws, and let go of the tension in your body. Close your eyes and imagine that you're surrounded by protective, supportive, and compassionate energy. This shield of energy glows in blue light, representing the presence of Archangel Michael. Imagine that you inhale some of this energy with each breath you take. Visualize it filling and blessing your body, giving you strength, peace, and wisdom. You can communicate your thoughts and feelings and express your gratitude toward the archangel during the meditation. Keep your mind and heart open to receive any messages that he might deliver.

Praying to the Archangel can facilitate the connection and strengthen your relationship with him. You can either recite prayers out loud or in your head. You can look up prayers dedicated to Archangel Michael or allow your intuition to guide you as you create your own. You can simply express your desires and explain your struggles to the Archangel. Thank him for taking the time to listen, offer his help, and be clear about your intentions. You can also repeat affirmations that embody the protection, courage, strength, and other qualities of the archangel. Make sure you can inhale the aroma of the essential oil throughout your practice.

Express your gratitude after you've completed the practice and slowly bring yourself back to the present moment. Communicate that you're willing to get in touch with him again and consistently work on strengthening your bond. Thoroughly reflect on your spiritual experience and anything unusual you might have noticed. Journal about any messages you received, insights you've made, or thoughts and feelings that surfaced during the practice. Think about how Archangel Michael's presence and guidance resonate with certain aspects of your life.

What steps can you take to incorporate his guidance and insights into your life? What would you change about this practice the next time you connect with the archangel? Is there anything that you haven't gained clarity about?

Essential Oils to Connect with Archangel Michael

Angelica

This essential oil's name is derived from the word "angel" because it has high vibrational frequencies. Incorporating it into your spiritual and meditative practices will give you strength, make you more focused, enhance your stamina and comfort, and allow you to feel grounded. You can use it if you wish to manifest spiritual support, healing, and bravery and ask for Archangel Michael's protection.

Basil

This essential oil is ideal if you wish to balance your chakra system and encourage your mind, body, and soul to fall into alignment. You should use it if you feel like you have fallen out of touch with your environment and reality and need help guiding your attention toward the bigger picture. Working with Basil reminds you of your soul's purpose and spiritual essence. It bridges between mundane and spiritual realities. This oil encourages better self and spiritual awareness, a deeper understanding of physical and otherworldly realities, and intuitive awakening.

Cinnamon

Work with cinnamon essential oil if you're struggling with negative thoughts and feelings. It will help you manifest positivity and happiness and subdue anxiety, stress, and sadness. Use Cinnamon essential oil when you feel like you're less compassionate and giving than usual or haven't been able to express your love and gratitude toward others. Cinnamon oil will deepen your self-compassion and remind you that you're worthy and loved, as well.

Geranium or Rose Geranium

Many people underestimate the importance of acknowledging and comforting their inner child. This part of humans never falters, no matter how old they grow. Growing up, you might have encountered emotionally unsettling experiences that affect you to this day. Mental and emotional issues can keep you stuck in a low vibrational frequency, hindering your ability to effectively engage in spiritual practices and connect with otherworldly entities. You must get in touch with your inner child to resolve any emotional or mental issues caused by your past.

Geranium essential oil can help you connect with your inner child to release any emotional or mental blockages you are dealing with. This oil must be used and handled cautiously because it might trigger heavy emotional responses. Incorporating it into your practices facilitates your ability to call on Archangel Michael for reassurance and comfort. It will also give you insight into potential opportunities and risks you might encounter. The fact that this oil has a subtle, flowery, and sweet aroma is also a plus.

Sandalwood

Sandalwood essential oil can generally assist your spiritual endeavors. It helps you when entering meditative or trance states, which makes it easier to connect with higher energetic vibrations and reach out to your higher self. Sandalwood also encourages understanding and strengthens your bond with the rest of humanity. It allows you to feel present in both physical and spiritual worlds. Sandalwood essential oil also helps create a conducive environment for prayer, rituals, groundwork, and meditation.

Frankincense

This essential oil is a great addition to psychic or spiritual work, especially if you're still a beginner. Frankincense is a protective essential oil that will prevent you from entering mental states or energetic frequencies that you're not ready to deal with yet. It also strips negative energies away from users, allowing them to enhance their spiritual frequency and gradually preparing them for higher and more profound connections. It's naturally aligned with otherworldly matters, making it the go-to aroma for calling for Archangel Michael's help. Frankincense is also effective for expressing your gratitude toward spiritual entities and sending them your prayers. This essential oil leads to better emotional regulation and compassion. It makes you more understanding of others and accepting of your environment.

Myrrh

Myrrh essential oil delves into the inner workings of the soul and the human psyche, where countless emotional and mental challenges exist. Nothing pulls you back as holding onto situations that are out of your control, regrets, and emotional wounds. Working with myrrh, however, gives you the strength you need to move on and forgive yourself and others. It offers the inner peace and sense of calm you need to approach decisions with clarity and untie the knots in your mind, heart, and soul. This essential oil helps you physically relax and unwind, as well. Resting your body is essential if you wish to make material, emotional, mental, and spiritual progress. Like frankincense, myrrh fosters compassion, acceptance, and compassion. Use it in your meditations to facilitate spiritual enlightenment and nurture your psychic abilities.

Orange

This oil revitalizes the mind, spirit, and soul. It makes your heart full and happy. Orange essential oil has an energizing essence that encourages transformation and regeneration. Using it regularly in your aromatherapy can help you overcome your obsessions and fears. Those working in creative and innovative fields can benefit from this aroma because it boosts your imagination and unleashes your creative skills. Orange essential oil also brings the joyful and inspiring presence of Archangel Michael into your daily life.

Rosemary

Reach for essential rosemary oil if you feel lost on your spiritual journey. It can bring your attention to knowledge and insights you have overlooked and will remind you of the very essence of your being. Rosemary keeps you grounded and cognizant that you're ultimately a spiritual being inhabiting a physical body to explore, enjoy, and learn from mundane experiences. It is an all-purpose oil that purifies your body and space and invokes the healing, protective, guiding, and compassionate nature of the angels.

Peppermint

This essential oil can push your spirit toward opportunities for deeper understanding. Working with it, you'll learn to appreciate everything in your life and recognize that everything happens for a purpose. Peppermint teaches you to patiently wait for the truth to unfold. This essential oil has a soothing effect on the mind and body. It keeps negative thoughts at bay while uplifting your overall aura. Peppermint aromatherapy makes you more perceptive and receptive. It makes you more sensitive to angelic messages and connection attempts. Use this oil to improve your self-awareness and alertness, even in your unconscious mental states. This will allow you to expand your knowledge and reflect on the wisdom you acquire from the spiritual realm.

Essential oils are among the most powerful and effective tools you can use to enhance your spiritual practices. You can experience substantial spiritual growth and development if you learn how to carefully select the right essential oils for your needs, set clear intentions for invocation, and use them correctly for their intended purpose. While you can't rely on essential oils to transform your overall health and wellbeing, you can use them to support your holistic self-care routine. Make sure to test for sensitivity and allergies before you apply them to your skin.

Chapter 9: Daily Rituals

Due to their far-reaching power, the abilities of Archangels reach all of humanity and every last individual life. Though Michael isn't a personal guardian angel, he is always available to aid you in any way necessary, regardless of the circumstance. He is a high-frequency being of light and energy, capable of supporting you at any time. However, asking him for help whenever needed and expressing your gratitude for his blessings aren't the only ways to form a connection with him. To build a deeper bond, you must nurture it through daily practices. Remember, he is there to watch over you. But he won't intervene unless he really needs to.

To work with him regularly, you must maintain an active line of communication between the two of you. Even dedicating 5-10 minutes a day to this purpose is enough. You can ask Michael to be with you, sit with you, or accompany you when you're spending time with your friends and family. It doesn't just have to be for healing, guidance, or warding off negative energies either. You can invoke him to keep you and your loved ones company. He is a protector. He will be happy to spend time looking over everyone you ask him to. Through this process, you will develop your connection with him, get to know him better, and hone your intuition to better decipher his messages. This final chapter provides some useful tips and rituals for connecting with Archangel Michael, like prayers, meditations, and wearing items associated with him.

Morning Affirmations with Archangel Michael

Archangel Michael is there to support your experience from the time you wake up until you fall asleep and sometimes even after. However, your mind is freshest and most relaxed right when you wake up after a good night's sleep, so this is the best time to address Michael. You can ask him to bless you with his protective light and love or guide you through your day if you're expecting to run into some challenges.

Here is an affirmation that will help you invoke Michael's energy and feel his presence throughout your day:

"*I* feel blessed by the Archangel Michael's love and light.

I feel the loving presence of Michael watching over me.

Today, I ask for guidance and the courage to act on it.

I seek harmony and peace to fill my life and to follow me throughout my day.

Today, I ask for guidance in making better choices,

So, I can become and express the best version of myself.

I thank you, Michael, for accompanying me throughout this day."

As you say this affirmation day after day, you'll feel your bond with Archangel Michael growing, getting more formidable, and filled with light. Your intuition will grow, allowing you to gain greater awareness of his presence and trust in the guidance he provides. When you ask him to accompany you, do it with a positive mindset and knowing that he will fully be there. Your mornings might be hectic, but Michael will be there to help. He will ensure that you're filled with serenity and joy and that you know you have the power to take control of the chaos.

Morning Healing with Archangel Michael

One of the main prerequisites of having a healthy mind is having a healthy body. For this, you'll need a good night's sleep to avoid rushing and have a great start to your day. When you wake up, make time for a healthy routine and a ritual dedicated to Archangel Michael. Whether you go for a healthy breakfast or a vitalizing lemon water, you can simply ask the Archangel to bless it for you. Just hold it in front of you, and ask him to purify it. Imagine him cleansing it with his light. This way, you can take advantage of its health benefits even more. It will nourish every cell in your body with positive energy, keeping your health and overall wellbeing in check.

Greeting the Sun

Greeting the sun is another empowering way to invoke Michael's energy, as he is associated with its nurturing warmth.

This is how easy it is to make this your morning ritual:

1. As you rise from your bed, turn towards the window (open it if it's closed and the weather permits). Or better yet, walk outside to your balcony or garden.
2. Look up to the sky (not directly into the sun), and say the following:

   "I greet you, Archangel Michael, the ruler of the magnificent sun.

   The Chief of Archangels and the Prince of Heavenly Army.

   May your light shine on me today,

   As the sun *does this morning."*
3. Feel the sun's energy permeating through your body.
4. Ask Michael for guidance or protection by sending out a silent request to him or by simply making it your intention for the day.
5. Thank the Archangel and return to your preparation for the day.

Archangel Michael Tea Ritual

What better way to honor Archangel Michael on a Sunday afternoon than with an invigorating cup of tea? You can use flowers or herbs associated with him or any special blend that makes you feel empowered every time you drink it.

Instructions:

1. Make your tea and ask Archangel Michael to bless it.
2. Light incense that makes you feel at peace and grounded. There are ready-made tea blends you can buy, but the ones you make yourself will have a much more powerful effect.
3. Thank Michael in advance for his guidance and blessings.

4. Drinking tea enriched with his light will help you get in touch with your higher self, listen to your intention, and become aware of angelic messages you might receive in the near future.

Daily Grounding Meditation

Take five minutes and do a healing breath meditation with Archangel Michael. He has incredibly restorative effects on your mind, body, and spirit. Whether you need empowerment to heal from a trauma or want to remain healthy, Michael can help you achieve your goals. You can do this at any time of the day.

Instructions:
1. Find a comfortable position in a secluded spot.
2. Have some soft music playing in the background, or enjoy the serenity of silence, whichever you prefer.
3. Ask Archangel Michael to release any energetic blocks you have.
4. Become aware of the sensation of the air going in and out of your nose for five minutes.
5. Any time your mind starts to wander while you're focusing on your breath, simply bring it back to the sensation of cool air going in and warmer air flowing out of your lungs.
6. End the meditation by thanking Michael and bringing yourself back to the room.
7. Enjoy having a clear head as you make or set in motion your plans for the day.

Goal Setting Ritual

The best way to ensure that you'll be able to stick to your goals is to set them while Archangel Michael is guiding you. He can help you set goals that contribute to your life's goals, making it easier to accomplish them regardless of the obstacles you might encounter along the way. Whenever you want to determine short or long-term targets, think of Archangel Michael, and invoke him silently. Whether it's a to-do list for the day or week or landing a promotion, it will be much easier to remain disciplined until you reach the goal if you know that Michael is there to guide and protect you through the process. Alternatively, you can summon him to empower your daily workouts as part of your healing journey.

Guidance Ritual

You'll find the following ritual helpful if you want to receive guidance from Archangel Michael. For example, you can ask him to help you protect yourself and others, release you from fear and unwanted ties, or even discover the truth behind something.

Instructions:
1. Walk for at least 15 minutes, preferably outdoors, where you can be closer to nature. During that time, think about everything you're thankful for in your life. This could be as simple as feeling the sunlight on your cheeks that morning, the smell of fresh air, the chirping of birds, or something as touching as the warm smile of your loved ones.
2. Return home, find a comfortable chair, and sit with your feet touching the ground. Then, close your eyes, and go over the list of blessings that you felt grateful for during your walk.
3. Have a clear picture of these blessings in your mind. Now, set the intention of calling upon Archangel Michael. Ask him for his approval before you proceed. There's a strong chance you will receive advice on changing the course of your thoughts at this point. If you do, listen to it, and act accordingly.
4. When you feel you can proceed, Take a few slow, deep breaths before exhaling slowly. Then, address Michael with the following words:

    *"Bless*ed Archangel Michael

    I am grateful for all the blessings in my life.

    Thank you for your guidance, healing, and love.

    I ask *you to join me now, as I need your help again."*
5. Pause for a minute. If you've felt the Archangel's supporting presence, you can continue. Otherwise, repeat your request as many times as necessary.
6. Don't worry if you don't receive a response right away. If you've expressed your concern clearly enough, Michael will know how and when to help you. His help might come when you least expect it, so be prepared to receive a message from

him at any point throughout the day. For example, if you performed this ritual before going to bed, you might receive a sign from him in the morning or in your dreams.
7. Finish the ritual by thanking Archangel Michael for his guidance and support.

Heart Chakra Meditation

Chakra meditation doesn't need to be a deep, all-consuming exercise. Simply taking a few minutes to raise your awareness of your chakras and their energy once a day will do wonders in keeping your mind, body, and soul healthy. This will be particularly effective if you do it with Archangel Michael's help.

Instructions:
1. Sit or lie down in a place where you won't be disturbed and bring awareness of your connection to Archangel Michael.
2. Close your eyes, and take a deep breath. Make an *"Aaah"* sound as you release your breath. Repeat until you feel a vibration in the middle of your chest.
3. When you do, you'll know that the energy has touched your heart chakra, the center of compassion and love.
4. Once you feel your heart chakra vibrating at a higher frequency, take three deep breaths and continue saying, *"Aaah,"* as you exhale.
5. At the same time, visualize the energy filling your body through your heart chakra until you feel filled with divine love.
6. Visualize Archangel Michael standing tall in front of you with his flaming blue sword by his side. Once you can feel his presence by your side, forget about your breathing, and start talking to him.
7. Tell Michael everything you want to communicate to him at that moment, even if it's only gratitude for his blessings.
8. When you're done, thank the Archangel for joining you, let his image go, and slowly return to your present.

Wearing Items Associated with Archangel Michael

Michael is often depicted wearing a blue cloak or with his body and sword surrounded by an electric blue flame emanating divine energy. This alludes to Michael's association with the color blue, which you can use to honor him in your daily life. You can wear blue, purple, and red; these colors represent Michael's power, loving protection, and compassion, respectively. As you put on the clothes you'll wear in his honor, invoke his guidance and love. This will be particularly effective if you plan to wear those clothes to do something important, like a job interview. Michael supports your core beliefs, and by being represented through his colors, he will be part of any conversations you have about your values. He won't let intimidation, doubt, and fear hinder you, whether it's coming from you or others. You can also wear talismans and charms, symbolizing Michael's energy.

That said, you do not necessarily have to wear anything associated with Michael to harness the angel's powers. Sometimes, all it takes is to envision them on or around you. For example, when you feel surrounded by negative energy, you can quickly imagine yourself being enveloped by Michael's blue cloak, and you will sense the negativity dissipating.

If you want to ward off negativity and illness from your home, imagine little swords cutting the cord of negativity and chasing away ailments. Everyone and everything inside your home will be protected, and all you did to make that happen was invoke Michael's power for 5-10 minutes a day. Are you struggling with fears or phobias you desperately wish to overcome? Just imagine Michael standing beside you, telling you that you can overcome everything. For example, if you have a fear of public speaking, you can practice speaking while holding a feather and standing in front of the mirror for 5-10 minutes every day. While you do this, just focus on Michael's energy empowering you.

Using Archangel Michael Talismans

If you're looking for a more hands-on daily ritual to honor Archangel Michael, the following one might be right for you. It incorporates gemstones and items associated with this angel. Depending on your purpose, use any of the colors corresponding to Michael, from blue to purple to red. Alternatively, you can use yellow or gold (to represent him as the governor of the sun) or white (to simply invoke universal divine power).

Instructions:
1. Make yourself comfortable, close your eyes, and take the item or items that you've chosen to use into your hands.
2. Take 3-5 slow, deep breaths, and then ask Archangel Michael to join you. If you're using more than one item, repeat this for each one.
3. Focus on the sensations you have when holding the item(s). You might notice a difference in their energies. Or, you might become aware that the angel is with you by feeling a warm, tingling sensation all over your body.
4. If you don't feel any feedback, try again. If nothing happens right away, don't worry. You might receive a message later on that day or the next one.

Thanking Archangel Michael

As part of your daily ritual to honor him, you should take a few minutes to thank Archangel Michael for all his blessings. You don't need to have any specific reason to summon him. You can reach out and thank him for the challenges he helped you overcome. For example, before going to bed, you can say:

"Thank you, Archangel Michael, for keeping me safe today.
Thank you for making me feel protected,
And bring me inner peace at the end of this day."

Imagining Archangel Michael Dispel Evil Influences

Suppose you ever feel troubled by negative energetic influences throughout your day. In that case, you can ask Archangel Michael to help you dispel them. Do this before going to bed; the angel will work for you overnight, allowing you to wake up free of negativity the following day.

Instructions:
1. Light a candle, sit in front of it, and close your eyes.
2. In your mind's eye, imagine Archangel Michael holding his sword, reaching out to you. See him cutting away negativity from your life, giving you the strength and protection you need.
3. Next, picture him catching all that negativity he cut out from your life in a white net, trapping it forever so it would return to your side.
4. Take a deep breath, release it, and you'll feel lighter.
5. Thank Archangel Michael, snuff out the candle, and go to bed.

Ask Archangel Michael for Help

You can ask Archangel Michael for help with anything you struggle with; he will be happy to help you. It's an effective morning or evening ritual for warding off any fears keeping you from living your life to the fullest. Keep in mind that the help might come in unexpected ways (like him staying away and sending encouragement to ensure you can do it on your own), but he will always empower you spiritually.

Instructions:
1. Find a secluded space to address Michael. Invoke him by chanting his name either aloud or silently in your mind.
2. Then, ask him whatever you wish to request. This can be as simple as granting you a safe journey on your vacation or business trip, helping you conduct an emotionally challenging conversion with your loved one, or keeping you and anyone you cherish safe during a storm.
3. Thank Michael for his assistance in advance, and continue with your daily activities.

Journaling with Archangel Michael

Journaling is another highly effective way of maintaining your connection with Archangel Michael. By thinking about what you wish to say, you're already focusing your energies on your bond with him. By writing it down, you're creating a tangible record of your connection to him. While he doesn't need to see your words, they will help you see your progress as your bond develops and you learn to work with him effectively. With enough practice, you might even notice Michael answering you while you're still writing your message, which will establish an active line of communication.

Instructions:

1. Take your journal and find a quiet place where you can focus on what you wish to write. You can pen down any request for resolving problems involving you or someone close to you. Or, you can simply note down what is on your mind. This is an excellent exercise for the night as it helps you organize and calm your thoughts, so they won't bother you during the night.

2. Sit straight, with your shoulders relaxed and your feet planted firmly on the round. This will help you feel grounded and close to nature. There is no faster way to connect to Michael than to the universal energy of nature that courses through all beings.

3. Take a few deep breaths. When you feel your energy settling down and your mind centering around your intention, continue.

4. Ask Archangel Michael to join you and start writing. Make sure to address him as a friend while you write. Don't worry about whether your writing makes sense, is in chronological order, or is grammatically correct. The goal is to clarify any problems you might have and resolve them with Michael's help.

5. Finish your thoughts by thanking Michael for reading your messages. Close your eyes and light a candle. Think about your inquiry, feel free to say anything else you wish Michael to know, and then snuff out the candle flame.

6. As you watch the candle smoke, carry your message to Michael, thank him again, and go to bed. You can be sure you'll hear back from Archangel Michael when the time is right.

Bonus: Correspondences Sheet

This bonus chapter includes all the correspondences associated with Archangel Michael.

The Day of the Week

Given his association with the Sun, Michael's corresponding day of the week is Sunday. This is the day when his powers are the greatest and when it's best to invoke him. Depending on your preferences, you can honor him on Sundays with prayers, meditations, and rituals dedicated to him or any intention he can assist you with. On Sundays, Michael can help you face painful truths, protect yourself from harmful influences and heal yourself through rest and spiritual elevation.

Festivals and Feasts

There are several days of the year associated with Michael. One of the most prominent is Michaelmas, a feast celebrated on the 29th of September in the Western part of the world. This tradition originates from Phrygia, Turkey. The Roman Catholic Church celebrates Archangel Michael on the 8th of May, the day known as the Apparition of St. Michael. According to ancient lore, St. Michael appeared on Mount Gargano in 492. The place has become a medieval pilgrimage site, and the feast of the apparition was born. The Eastern Orthodox Church honors the Archangel as St. Michael on the 8th of November. Meanwhile, the Ethiopian Orthodox Tewahedo Church commemorates this angel on the 12th of each month.

Zodiac Signs

Archangel Michael is the ruler of Leo, the zodiac sign embodying the characteristics of those born under the rule of the Sun. Leos are known for their excellent communication skills and a powerful drive to protect and help those in need. Inspired by Michael, those born under the sign of Leo have no trouble uncovering hidden truths and are in constant pursuit of knowledge that can help them improve themselves. They're always open to new ideas and capable of acknowledging other peoples' beliefs and values, just as Archangel Michael accepts the opinions of anyone willing to work with him. A typical Leo won't judge and demands the same from those around them.

Michael gives Leos an incredible ability to focus and persevere, organize their lives, and use these skills to earn recognition. Because their efforts are often recognized, Leos learn to thrive on success and will always seek to be in the limelight. They are prepared to give the very best of themselves to obtain credit and acclaim. Empowered by Archangel Michael, a Leo will always stand out from the competition. While they often only seek individual success, they will remain generous toward those who helped them.

Michael teaches Leos how to nurture loyalty, love, and compassion, making them warm and sincere individuals who are never afraid to show affection, just as Michael isn't afraid to show love toward his devotees. He also gives Leos self-assurance, allowing them to believe they can overcome any obstacle they face.

In some cases, Leos can be overly proud and egotistical. They might gravitate towards extravagant gestures and showing off their accomplishments before realizing the error of their ways.

Planets

Sun

Out of all the planetary bodies, Archangel Michael is primarily associated with the Sun. In astrology, the Sun determines the most prominent characteristics of each zodiac sign. Under Michael's influence, the Sun helps each sign develop its most basic identity. This forms a person's core identity, the inner place all your personality traits are centered around.

The Sun also determines characteristics like dignity, authority, ambition, resilience towards prejudice, self-awareness, non-conformity, and staying true to your values. To prevent these traits from turning into an overwhelming desire for power, inability to accept other peoples' ideas, lack of will, intolerance towards rules, pride, self-centeredness, and recklessness, Michael (through the Sun) keeps people on the right track. He nurtures people's positive traits, just as the Sun nurtures life on Earth.

Mercury

Mercury is the planet of communication, something at which Archangel Michael excels. He isn't afraid to voice his opinion or stand up for those who can't do the same. Those affected by Mercury can also experience some of Michael's influence when trying to express their desires and their inner world. It also helps develop one's ability to maximize consciousness when learning to discern and correctly interpret reality. Mercury is linked to traits like ingenuity, impartiality, multitasking, adaptability, and the ability to put spiritual exercises into practice. It promotes the union between one's personality and the spiritual realm.

Mars

The red planet, as Mars is known, corresponds to traits like commitment to self-improvement and the ability to overcome obstacles and fears that might hinder your progress and keep you stuck in an undesirable position. These are all characteristics bestowed by Archangel Michael, who ensures you learn how to dissolve everything that stagnates inside and prevents you from becoming the best version of yourself. Under Michael's influence, Mars can bring rapid changes, but it all goes in the right direction. Those affected by this planet often have a sudden urge to start working toward self-realization after fully grasping their present situations and acknowledging that they're stuck. They often switch into a higher gear, empowered by the truth and their ability to nurture their own spiritual strength.

Earth

Due to his ability to nurture life on Earth, Archangel Michael is also associated with it. Representing a symbol of Earth can be a great way of empowering one's connection with nature and the birthplace of humanity.

Angel Number

While Michael can manifest through several numbers, he often gravitates toward the numbers 1, 11, and 1111. Number 1 is incredibly prominent in the world of angels. If Michael is using this number (or combinations of it) to reach out to you, he has a significant message to deliver.

First and foremost, number 1 is linked to the one true self, which you can reach through your intuition. If you're seeing this number, it can indicate that you need to tap into your gut feelings. If you see the number 11, this means you have an elevated spiritual energy. It's a sign that you're receptive to spiritual messages. Messages linked to number 11 are often about the protection of your loved ones. Unlike number 1 (which is linked to your personal intuition), number 11 is more about using your intuition to help others. Some also believe that the number 11 depicts two tall figures, indicating that the Archangel will always stand with you.

If you keep encountering the number 1111, this could also be Michael's way of communicating with you. Never ignore this number because it can hold a message that could change your life. Michael can be incredibly persistent, and if you can't pick up on any other signs he is sending your way, he might start bombarding you with the number 1111 until you have no choice but to notice he is trying to deliver a message.

Another number you'll see when Michael is reaching out to you is 888. This represents Michael's connection to the divine. It's the triplicity of the number 8, the symbol of power, worldly status, and leadership. 888 can be reduced to 6, the number linked to the divine energy of service and another number associated with Archangel Michael. When he sends you the number 888, he reminds you of your responsibilities and the cause-and-effect relationship. He is telling you that every action has consequences. He often sends this number to help you understand the importance of integrity, staying true to your values, and all the steps you need to achieve this. Number 8 is also said to symbolize the divine sword of Archangel Michael. In triplicity, the symbol of the sword embodies the protection you need to live a righteous life, allowing you to grow through your interactions with spiritual power, responsibilities, and decisions, and the lack thereof.

The number 36 might be Michael's way of signaling that you must shift your focus in certain areas of life. If this number appears to you repeatedly, it can be a cue to stop focusing on outside values and to channel your attention to your inner self. Perhaps you're too focused on material possessions and financial gains. Seeing the number 36 can signify that you're ready for a spiritual journey that will make you lose focus on these concerns.

Colors

Archangel Michael is connected to several colors:

- **Blue** - The symbol of his protection, blue is often associated with serenity. It conveys calmness in the middle of chaos, allowing you to overcome obstacles.
- **Gold** - This color represents Michael's power as the Archangels' leader and the Sun's governor. Michael often appears in visions in his majestic form, enveloped in an aura of sparkling golden light.
- **Red** - Michael's association with the color of love alludes to his compassionate nature and ability to teach people how to develop love toward themselves and others and nurture this sentiment.
- **Purple** - Purple combines blue and red, indicating the Archangel's ability to provide loving protection. Purple symbolizes royalty, alluding to Michael's distinguished status among the Archangels.
- **Green** - Michael's abilities are linked to nature, best represented by the color green. Green has a grounding effect, helping to soothe and center one's mind during spiritual work.
- **White** - Michael's magnificent energy is often depicted by the universal angelic color, white. It can be helpful if you don't have a specific intention in mind or when or need all the power Michael can provide.

Symbol, Seal, and Sigil

Archangel Michael is frequently depicted carrying a sword, which has become one of his signature symbols of protection. Devotees often visualize his protective energy through his sword or simply through an orb of light. The sword and the light are either blue or surrounded by blue flame. These two angelic symbols represent Michael's ability to shield and protect you from harmful energies, cut unwanted ties, and free you from falsehood, allowing you to see the truth.

Michael is also attributed to other protection symbols, like the hexagram and pentagram, both of which are used in spiritual and magical work in different religions. Similarly to a shield, a cloak can also be Michael's symbol, especially if it's blue or royal purple. Some also prefer using representations of the sun as Michael's symbol. It depicts the Archangel's nurturing energy, which can come in handy during spiritual healing.

The sigil (also known as the seal of St. Michael) of Archangel Michael is a highly regarded religious emblem among followers of a wide variety of religions. While there are many different versions of the sigil, most devotees agree that it's best used to establish a bond between the Archangel and the person who wants to work with him regularly.

Trees, Plants, Herbs, and Essential Oils

As the Archangel associated with the highest power of angelic healing, Michael has many herbs, flowers, and essential oils in his apothecary. Some corresponding plants for Michael are acacia, angelica, beech, buttercup, blueweed, bay, cedar, hickory, carnation, sunflower, laurel, celandine, lovage, centaury, eyebright, goldenseal, heliotrope, hops, hibiscus, marigold, orange blossoms, peony, oak, rowan, basil, saffron, St. John's wort, sunflower, and tagetes.

To point out a few honorable mentions, basil is linked to Archangel Michael due to their mutual ability to banish negativity. It was once considered a powerful healing herb used by royalty. It can also be used in essential oil form to cleanse spaces and bodies before rituals and prayers dedicated to Michael. Other essential oils corresponding to Michael are orange and frankincense. They, too, can be used as prayer oils, anointments, and spritzers when invoking Michael's power for protection, strength, and peace of mind.

Solar-shaped blooms, flowers with a citrusy scent, and flowers that improve sight also work well when invoking Archangel Michael. As its name implies, the sunflower is one of Michael's correspondences. Using it can be a great way to honor Michael as the governor of the sun. Besides, the sunflower is also said to symbolize trust and faith in spirituality and the divine.

Incenses associated with Archangel Michael are lavender and frankincense. The former has a cleansing and soothing effect on your entire being while cleansing out your energies. The latter promotes calmness and purges the room of negative vibes and energetic influences.

Crystals and Metals

Archangel Michael is mainly associated with purple and blue gemstones, crystals, and stones. The deep purple sugilite has a particularly strong connection to this Archangel. Michael is also linked to topaz, amber, and several yellow, yellowish brown colored crystals, as well as blue stones like aqua aura and turquoise. You can also get great results when invoking Michael with gold and brass metal items. These metals have a high energy signature, just like the angel ruling them. Steel can also be used to summon Michael, as this metal is associated with his immense powers of protection.

Other Associations of Archangel Michael

The hour of the day and night: Michael governs the 1st and 8th hours of the day and the 3rd and 10th hours of the night.

Direction: West

Element: Fire

Tarot card: The Sun

Deities: Helios, Sol, Apollo, Thor, Adonis, Ra, Savitar, Re, and Sekhmet

Animals and mythical creatures: Lion, griffin, wolf, sparrowhawk, and golden butterfly.

Body Parts: The heart and the circulatory system, eyes, spinal column, spleen, upper back, blood.

Chakra system: Heart chakra (Anahata) and crown chakra (Sahasrara).

Spiritual correspondences: Peace, worldly ambition, financial gains, seeking employment, favors gained from others, ability to regain one's youth, acquire good luck and recover something or someone lost. Michael is known to help with business ventures, promotions, establishing mutually satisfying partnerships, and a path toward professional success. He is also linked to health, personal growth and advancement, joy, enlightenment, spiritual prosperity, hope, rational thinking, dispelling negative energies, and resolution of short-term or long problems.

Personal traits and skills: Personal characteristics governed by Archangel Michael are leadership skills, nobility, the ability to establish successful careers, reverence toward the law and rules, being a good role model as a father figure, and in friendships. He is also linked to self-confidence, ego, physical traits, ability to resolve hostile situations, ego, seeking fame, honor, life-bringing energy, spiritual lightness, success, vitality, superiority, virility, power promotion, and pride.

Conclusion

Archangel Michael is known for being a protector and the source of sacred empowerment for angels and people alike. As you've learned from this book, he is the Archangel closest to the divine. However, he is also the governor of the sun, providing nature with his nourishing energy. He protects those who can't speak for themselves and shields those in danger of evil influences. He can help you heal your body and mind by empowering your spirit and overcoming any difficulties you face in life. Whether it's through healing your chakras, bringing you closer to nature, or aligning you with your life's purpose, Michael will elevate your spirits and help you become the best version of yourself.

Suppose this is your first time working with an angelic being. In that case, you'll probably need a little practice establishing a clear communication line with Archangel Michael. After taking the first step and contacting him, you must watch for signs of him. The great thing about Michael is that he is always direct and persistent. With patience, you will eventually recognize his signs.

After that, it will be time to make specific inquiries. Throughout this book, you've received plenty of tips and practical advice for requesting protection, healing, and banishing negative energies. Whether you want to protect yourself, your loved ones, or your possessions from toxic influences, Michael will help you out. You can ask for his assistance during spiritual work or if you simply feel worn down by negative vibes. You can also ask him to dispel all the negativity that already resides in any space, item, or person you want to purify. Negative energies can cause physical, mental, and spiritual distress. By eliminating them with the help of Archangel Michael, you can be sure that they won't return anytime soon. While he can't cure any physical and mental illnesses, Michael can give you strength to allow your mind, body, and soul to heal. Working with Michael can be a superb complementary exercise for any treatment you undergo.

Do you want to form an even stronger bond with Archangel Michael? You can do it by incorporating elements to honor him into your day-to-day life. For example, you can use crystals associated with him to harness his energy. Stones charged with Archangel Michael's energy can be a great source of empowerment to get you through daily challenges. They can also aid you during any spiritual work you dedicate to Michael. Likewise, you can also find power in herbs and essential oils associated with this Archangel, and those are just as easy to incorporate into daily practices.

Even if you don't have items associated with Michael at hand, visualize a symbol associated with him, and he will hear your request. The relevant chapter provided you with a broad range of correspondences linked to this Archangel - feel free to refer to any of them while working with him. Simply wearing adequately colored clothes or addressing him on the day his powers are strongest can make a big difference in your ability to connect with him.

All in all, you've received plenty of advice on how to connect to Archangel Michael. Now it's up to you to begin your journey. Remember, practice makes perfect. You might not be able to decipher any messages you receive from Archangel Michael initially, but this will change over time. As you raise your energies to higher frequencies and become more attuned to your intuition, you'll learn how to get the most out of your connection with him.

Here's another book by Mari Silva that you might like

Your Free Gift
(only available for a limited time)

Thanks for getting this book! If you want to learn more about various spirituality topics, then join Mari Silva's community and get a free guided meditation MP3 for awakening your third eye. This guided meditation mp3 is designed to open and strengthen ones third eye so you can experience a higher state of consciousness. Simply visit the link below the image to get started.

https://spiritualityspot.com/meditation

References

(N.d.-a). Questionsonislam.com. https://questionsonislam.com/question/what-are-duties-mikail-michael-did-he-see-and-talk-prophet-pbuh

(N.d.-b). Chabad.org. https://www.chabad.org/library/article_cdo/aid/3825092/jewish/What-Are-Archangels.htm

11 Steps To Connect With Archangel Michael. (2019, July 11). Georgie G Deyn. https://www.georgiegdeyn.com/11-steps-connect-archangel-michael/

5 Easy Ways. (2022, April 22). The Quantum Lab. https://www.newworldblueprints.com/how-to-communicate-with-archangel-michael/

6 Undeniable Signs Archangel Michael is Connecting to You – Angel Readings, Angel Healings, Psychic Medium. (2021, October 4). Angel Readings, Angel Healings, Psychic Medium. https://archangelwisdom.com/6-undeniable-signs-archangel-michael-is-connecting-to-you/

7 Angelic Morning Rituals. (2015, April 15). Angelorum. https://angelorum.co/topics/angels/7-morning-rituals-to-infuse-your-day-with-angelic-energy/

7 Signs Archangel Michael Could Be Your Personal Healer. (2021, January 15). Archangel Secrets. https://www.archangelsecrets.com/7-signs-st-michael-the-archangel-healer/

888 Angel Number and Angel Michael. (2020, July 9). AskAstrology.

A Daily Angel Routine – New Age. (n.d.). Bellaonline.Com. http://www.bellaonline.com/articles/art38477.asp

Angel, A. (n.d.). Archangel Michael. Circleofangels.Nl. https://circleofangels.nl/?page_id=2038

Angels and essential oils. (2017, April 3). S.O.N.C.E. https://spiritualyopeningnowtocosmicenergy.wordpress.com/angels-and-essential-oils/

Archangel Michael – He who is like God Angel. (2021, March 16). Unifycosmos.com. https://unifycosmos.com/archangel-michael/

Archangel Michael, Archangel of the Sun – Traditional Magical Correspondences. (n.d.). Archangels-and-Angels.Com. http://www.archangels-and-angels.com/aa_pages/correspondences/angel_planet/archangel_michael.html

Archangel Michael. (n.d.). Angelwingsart.Co.Uk. https://www.angelwingsart.co.uk/archangel-michael.php

Archangelic Flower Correspondences. (2022, August 8). Angelorum. https://angelorum.co/angels-2/angel-mystic-monday/archangelic-flower-correspondences/

Askinosie, H. (2016, February 5). 8 ways to use crystals in your everyday routine. Mindbodygreen. https://www.mindbodygreen.com/articles/how-to-use-crystals-everyday

August. (2020, August 30). Scientific facts about wearing gemstones – Hubert jewelry – fine diamonds and gemstones. Hubertjewelry.com. https://hubertjewelry.com/scientific-facts-about-wearing-gemstones/

Brandstatter, T. (2013, May 25). Guardian angels in the orthodox faith. Synonym.com; Synonym. https://classroom.synonym.com/guardian-angels-in-the-orthodox-faith-12087290.html

Brown, S. (2018, September 7). Who is Archangel Michael? Overcome fear with the Archangel of Courage. The Black Feather Intuitive. https://www.theblackfeatherintuitive.com/who-is-archangel-michael-the-archangel-of-courage/

Catholic Online. (n.d.). St. Michael the Archangel. Catholic Online. https://www.catholic.org/saints/saint.php?saint_id=308

Cheryl. (2017, October 25). 4 Ways to Connect with Archangel Michael (It's Easier than you Think!). Intuitive Journey. https://intuitivejourney.com/connect-archangel-michael/

Connect to Angels with Angel Mantras & the Power of Intention – Angel Readings, Angel Healings, Psychic Medium. (2021, September 6). Angel Readings, Angel Healings, Psychic Medium. https://archangelwisdom.com/connect-to-angels-angel-mantras/

Cotton, I. (2015, October 21). Think on these things: Book of Daniel's Michael is Jesus. Today In BC

Crystals to help connect with archangel Michael. (n.d.). Healingcrystals.com. https://www.healingcrystals.com/Crystals_to_Help_Connect_with_Archangel_Michael_Articles_1790.html

Dagny. (2016, September 3). Writing to Archangel Michael. Reiki Rays. https://reikirays.com/33506/writing-archangel-michael/

Deyn, G. G. (2019, July 11). 11 steps to connect with Archangel Michael. Georgie G Deyn. https://www.georgiegdeyn.com/11-steps-connect-archangel-michael/

Elias, A. A. (2021, April 4). Hadith on Mikaeel: Michael has not laughed since Hell was created. Daily Hadith Online. https://www.abuaminaelias.com/dailyhadithonline/2021/04/04/mikaeel-laughing/

Helen West, R. D. (2019, September 30). What are essential oils, and do they work? Healthline. https://www.healthline.com/nutrition/what-are-essential-oils

Hope - The Angel Writer. (2020, February 18). 6 Signs Archangel Michael Is Visiting You —. The Angel Writer. https://www.theangelwriter.com/blog/signs-archangel-michael

Hopler, W. (2011, May 20). Meet Archangel Michael, leader of all angels. Learn Religions. https://www.learnreligions.com/meet-archangel-michael-leader-of-angels-124715

Hopler, W. (2012a, January 1). Do you have your own guardian angel? Learn Religions. https://www.learnreligions.com/your-own-guardian-angel-123820

Hopler, W. (2012b, March 21). Archangels: God's leading angels. Learn Religions. https://www.learnreligions.com/archangels-gods-leading-angels-123898

Hopler, W. (2012c, May 1). Archangel Michael will lead the fight against Satan during end times. Learn Religions. https://www.learnreligions.com/bible-angels-archangel-michael-124047

Hopler, W. (2012d, May 1). How to recognize archangel Michael. Learn Religions. https://www.learnreligions.com/how-to-recognize-archangel-michael-124278

Hopler, W. (n.d.). How to Recognize Archangel Michael. Learn Religions. https://www.learnreligions.com/how-to-recognize-archangel-michael-124278

Hopler, W. (n.d.). How to Recognize Archangel Michael. Learn Religions. https://www.learnreligions.com/how-to-recognize-archangel-michael-124278

Hughes, L. (2019, March 1). What are healing crystals, and do they actually work? Oprah Daily. https://www.oprahdaily.com/life/health/a26559820/healing-crystals/

Hunter, M. G. (2022, November 11). Who is the archangel, Michael? Earth and Altar. https://earthandaltarmag.com/posts/who-is-the-archangel-michael

Incredible Personal Encounters with Saint Michael. (n.d.). Original Botanica. https://originalbotanica.com/blog/saint-michael-personal-encounter-stories

Insight Network, Inc. (n.d.). 21-Day Spiritual Cleansing With Archangel Michael. Insighttimer.Com. https://insighttimer.com/meditativeawakening/guided-meditations/21-day-spiritual-cleansing-with-archangel-michael

Insight Network, Inc. (n.d.). Archangel Michael Protection Meditation. Insighttimer.Com. https://insighttimer.com/gusferreira/guided-meditations/archangel-michael-protection-meditation

Insight Network, Inc. (n.d.). The Shield Of Michael Guided Visualisation. Insighttimer.Com. https://insighttimer.com/stevenobel/guided-meditations/the-shield-of-michael-meditation

ireneblais. (n.d.). Archangel Michael... – Angel Feathers Energy. Angelfeathersenergy.Ca. https://angelfeathersenergy.ca/2017/09/06/archangel-michael/

Khepri, V. A. P. by. (2012, August 19). Archangel Michael: How to Invoke His Help & Protection. The Magickal-Musings of Nefer Khepri, PhD. https://magickalmusings.blog/2012/08/19/archangel-michael-how-to-invoke-his-help-protection/

Khepri, V. A. P. by. (2015, May 15). Spiritual House Cleansing with Archangel Saint Michael. The Magickal-Musings of Nefer Khepri, PhD. https://magickalmusings.blog/2015/05/15/spiritual-house-cleansing-with-archangel-saint-michael/

Kranz, J. (2013, November 7). 7 biblical facts about Michael the archangel. OverviewBible. https://overviewbible.com/michael-archangel/

Lmhc, L. H. (1488904367000). Why Archangel Michael is the Ultimate Career Counselor. Linkedin.com. https://www.linkedin.com/pulse/why-archangel-michael-ultimate-career-counselor-lisa-hutchison-lmhc/

Lucey, C. (2022, April 6). Who is the Archangel Michael? Christianity.com. https://www.christianity.com/wiki/angels-and-demons/who-is-the-archangel-michael.html

Lundal, J. A. (2021, February 13). 7 Signs Archangel Michael Is Close. Spirit Miracle. https://www.spiritmiracle.com/signs-archangel-michael/

MacDougal, C. (2019, August 15). Crystals: The science behind the spiritual. ĀTHR Beauty. https://athrbeauty.com/blogs/goodvibesbeauty/crystals-the-science-the-spiritual

Malaikah. (n.d.). BBC. https://www.bbc.co.uk/bitesize/guides/z43pfcw/revision/3

Marie, T. (2019, January 17). How to use healing crystals & summon the Archangels you need most. YourTango. https://www.yourtango.com/experts/angellady-terriemarie/how-to-use-healing-crystals-to-connect-with-archangels-based-on-their-meanings

Michael the archangel. (2019, February 11). The Spiritual Life. https://slife.org/archangel-michael/

Michael, Wille, & Mary. (2021, May 10). Who Is Archangel Michael & 5 Sings of the Great Protector. A Little Spark of Joy. https://www.alittlesparkofjoy.com/archangel-michael/

Miller, F. P., Vandome, A. F., & McBrewster, J. (Eds.). (2010). Archangel Michael: Roman Catholic traditions and views. Alphascript Publishing.

Miller, F. P., Vandome, A. F., & McBrewster, J. (Eds.). (2010). Archangel Michael: Roman Catholic traditions and views. Alphascript Publishing.

Mishra, D. P. (2023, February 9). Angel Number 36 – A Complete Guide to Angel Number 36 Meaning and Significance. EAstroHelp. https://www.eastrohelp.com/blog/angel-number-36-meaning/

Murray, B., & March, B. (2017, September 5). A beginner's guide to crystals. Harper's BAZAAR. https://www.harpersbazaar.com/uk/beauty/fitness-wellbeing/a43244/crystal-healing-beginners-guide/

pakosloski. (2020, October 8). Prayer to St. Michael for protection against spiritual enemies. Aleteia — Catholic Spirituality, Lifestyle, World News, and Culture. https://aleteia.org/2020/10/08/prayer-to-st-michael-for-protection-against-spiritual-enemies/

Payment, D. (2017, May 11). Archangel Michael Protective Holy Water. Dar Payment - The Official Site of Psychic Medium, Author, and Spiritual Teacher Dar Payment. https://darpayment.com/archangel-michael-protective-holy-water/

Payment, D. (2017, November 3). Archangel Michael Room Purification Salt Recipe. Dar Payment - The Official Site of Psychic Medium, Author, and Spiritual Teacher Dar Payment. https://darpayment.com/archangel-michael-room-purification-salt-recipe/

Payment, D. (2020, February 3). All About Archangel Michael. Dar Payment - The Official Site of Psychic Medium, Author, and Spiritual Teacher Dar Payment. https://darpayment.com/all-about-archangel-michael/

Payment, D. (2020, February 3). All About Archangel Michael. Dar Payment - The Official Site of Psychic Medium, Author, and Spiritual Teacher Dar Payment. https://darpayment.com/all-about-archangel-michael/

Payment, D. (2022, May 27). Using Essential Oils to connect with angels. Dar Payment - The Official Site of Psychic Medium, Author, and Spiritual Teacher Dar Payment.

https://darpayment.com/using-essential-oils-to-connect-with-angels/

Plant, R. (2021, March 10). Michael Name Meaning. Verywell Family. https://www.verywellfamily.com/michael-name-meaning-5115812

Richardson, T. C., & Richardson, T. C. (n.d.). 5 ways Archangel Michael has your back – beliefnet. Beliefnet.com. https://www.beliefnet.com/inspiration/angels/5-ways-archangel-michael-has-your-back.aspx

Rose, M. (2022, December 8). StyleCaster. StyleCaster. https://stylecaster.com/how-to-use-protection-magic/

Rue. (2010, May 28). Protection Charm Charged With The Fire of Saint Michael the Archangel — Rue's Kitchen. Rue's Kitchen. https://www.rueskitchen.com/articles/protection-charm-charged-with-the-fire-of-saint-michael-the.html

Saint Michael's Day Rituals for Abundance and Protection. (n.d.). Original Botanica. https://originalbotanica.com/blog/saint-michaels-day-rituals-abundance-protection

Spiritual. (2016, January 18). Sigil Of Archangel Michael - How To Create It. Spiritual Experience

Stefan. (2021, April 25). Archangel Michael in the Reiki Session. Reiki Rays. https://reikirays.com/87365/archangel-michael-in-the-reiki-session/

The Archangel Michael—Who Is He? (n.d.). JW.ORG. https://www.jw.org/en/bible-teachings/questions/archangel-michael/

The Crystal Garden, South Florida's home for the holistic community. (n.d.). The Crystal Garden. https://thecrystalgarden.com/category/angels/

The Editors of Encyclopedia Britannica. (2020). Mīkāl. In Encyclopedia Britannica.

The Editors of Encyclopedia Britannica. (2022). Michael. In Encyclopedia Britannica.

The Editors of Encyclopedia Britannica. (2022). Michael. In Encyclopedia Britannica.

The word Michael mentioned in Quran. (2019, February 10). The Last Dialogue. https://www.thelastdialogue.org/article/the-word-michael-mentioned-in-quran/

View Archive →. (2023, April 11). Sigil of Archangel Michael: Meaning and Origin. Malevus. https://malevus.com/sigil-of-archangel-michael/

Waters, R. (2016, November 3). Crystals for the Archangels. Carpe Diem With Remi. https://www.carpediemwithremi.com.au/blogs/news/crystals-for-the-archangels

Webster, R. (2004, November 1). Contacting the Archangel Michael. Llewellyn Worldwide. https://www.llewellyn.com/journal/article/732

Webster, R. (2022, June 13). 7 ways to connect with archangels. Llewellyn Worldwide. https://www.llewellyn.com/journal/article/3023

Webster, R. (2022, June 13). 7 Ways to Connect with Archangels. Llewellyn Worldwide. https://www.llewellyn.com/journal/article/3023

Who is Saint Michael? (2019, December 23). Saint Michael's College. https://www.smcvt.edu/about-smc/who-is-saint-michael/

Wille. (2021, May 10). Who is Archangel Michael & 5 sings of the great protector. A Little Spark of Joy. https://www.alittlesparkofjoy.com/archangel-michael

Printed in Great Britain
by Amazon